Mission
accomplished

Mission accomplished

by

Michael Scott Horton

 EVANGELICAL PRESS

EVANGELICAL PRESS
12 Wooler Street, Darlington, Co. Durham, DL1 1RQ, England.

First published in the U.S.A. in 1986 by Thomas Nelson Inc.
First Evangelical Press edition 1990.

British Library Cataloguing in Publication Data available.

ISBN 0-85234-277-2

Typeset by Outset Studios, Hartlepool.
Printed in Great Britain at The Bath Press, Avon.

To Mom and Dad,
whose love for me and this
message kept me going

Contents

Acknowledgements

I would like to thank Jay Adams, James M. Boice, Carl F. H. Henry, D. James Kennedy, John MacArthur, Jr, Marilyn Meberg, Roger R. Nicole, Paige Patterson, J. I. Packer, Earl Radmacher, Ray. C. Stedman, R. C. Sproul and other guests appearing on the *Mission Accomplished* audio/video/film projects. Each of these people has graciously donated time, energy and advice to this effort.

I also want to thank Peter Gillquist, who has been as much a tutor as an editor. Special thanks go to the friends who have worked with Christians United for Reformation (CURE) on this project: John Melkonian, Mark Salo, Bruce Ryrie, Larry Johnson, Kari Olsen, Bob and Carol Williams, Pete Smeltzer and my close associate, Michael McGuire. Thanks too to my best friend, Clark Bowers, for his support.

Most importantly, my deepest appreciation goes to my family: my parents for enduring my incessant work on this project; my brothers Gary and Larry and my sister-in-law Linda, for their support. Included in my thanks to my family is my appreciation for Scott Sanborn, who has not only been my closest associate, but a brother without whom I could never have completed the project.

Most important of all, thanks to the Lord, who never gave up, even when I did.

Foreword

Once upon a time, people in the Christian world knew that the most important issues anyone faces are those of eternity. They knew that God the Creator is pure and holy, that we are in his hands and that one day we must give an account to him. They knew that none of us is naturally fit to do that, and that therefore the quest for salvation — not from our pain, misery, poverty and exploitation, but from the guilt and power of our sins — is life's top priority.

In those days the study of redemption was everyone's concern and God's plan of salvation was a matter of general interest. Today, however, it is not so.

Why is that? Not because the problem has ceased to exist. God and man are the same, and the need for salvation remains as acute as it ever was. At least four excuses keep people from seeking salvation.

Distraction is one reason. The issues of eternity are pushed out of our minds by the insistent pressures of the present. Our jet-propelled culture keeps us so busy with immediate concerns that we have no time to think of how we stand with God.

Preoccupation is another reason. Our interest is held by the material products and prospects of our technology, leaving no room for any care about spiritual and eternal issues.

Mythology is a third reason. (I use that word as sociologists do, meaning 'stories made up to sanctify social patterns'.) We are constantly told that Christianity is a thing of the past, having been exploded somehow by modern scientific and historical knowledge. The view that science has displaced Christianity is an established myth of our time.

Arrogance is a final reason. We are unwilling to believe

that any generation before our own was as wise as we are, let alone wiser, and therefore we decline on principle to accept anything from the past. Thus, with all our technological expertise, we end up the cleverest fools in world history, and the story of our era becomes the saddest tale of falling away from God and exchanging light for darkness that has ever been heard since the tragedy of Eden.

Mike Horton is a young man who has seen through all the excuses and who appreciates that true and timeless wisdom is found in the paths of the Christian gospel. *Mission accomplished* expresses the thrill of his soul — and mine — as we gaze upon the triumph of God's almighty grace through the life, death, resurrection, present reign and future return of the mediator, 'God incarnate, man divine,' our Lord and Saviour Jesus Christ.

Mike Horton says it the way the early Reformers, following the New Testament and Augustine, said it: sin has made us utterly impotent for real godliness in any shape or form; and it takes omnipotent mercy from the Father, Son and Holy Spirit to save us. This statement is right, as all believers will know in eternity even if they fail to see it clearly here on earth; and I commend most heartily Mike Horton's labour to make it clear, so that God may be praised on earth in the same terms that angels and triumphant saints are already using in heaven.

Here is the quintessence of the gospel, the new wine of God's kingdom at its purest for us today! Read, mark, learn and inwardly digest *Mission accomplished*.

J. I. Packer

1.
Why are we Christians, anyway?

Many times I have asked myself, 'Why am I a Christian?' I have never been content with the prefabricated answers I have received, and I am not so dishonest as to suppose I can claim a faith I do not understand to some degree. Humanly speaking, were it not for the message of the life-changing grace of God, I am certain that I would not be a Christian today.

In fact, I am convinced that the effectiveness of these truths is the only thing standing between me and the cynical scepticism in which many former churchgoers have found themselves. If you are wondering why you continue to call yourself a Christian, or are disillusioned with Christianity as you may see and hear it around you, take heart! For it is in the lives of people like us that the truth of God's grace is so effective.

In his book, *The Choice of Truth,* Daniel Thrapp wrote, 'The purpose of life is the quest for truth.'[1] I have always known that God had something to say and that he had said it in his Word. But, as my report cards would later attest, I had a restless side. I read nothing more intellectual than *MAD* magazine. I was not an academic. In fact, I was about twelve when I finally realized that studying was not a break from holidays, but the other way round.

The year I was twelve things began to change in my life — not all at once, but gradually. I had been involved in family devotions and Bible reading, but suddenly the Bible sprang to life for me. The book of Romans began to shatter many of my earlier notions about reality. Every time I read from Romans I found myself searching for a deeper understanding of God's purpose and grace.

After playing baseball each afternoon, I would come home, and pick up Romans, and go through it again and again. What I found in Romans had me mesmerized, and I began to share my discoveries with anyone who would listen. My parents were the owners of a nursing home, so I had a ready-made congregation. I began conducting weekly services that lasted, with brief interruptions, for six years (up to my senior year in high school). People who were not even residents attended the services to hear about God's effective grace.

The first concept to change my life was that I was declared righteous before God on the basis of what Christ had done, not what I had done. We all know that we are inadequate, that somehow we just don't meet God's standards. After reading the first part of Romans I was backed into a corner and felt the sting of despair; I could find no way out. I was forced to view myself as God viewed me — helpless and impotent, until his grace moved in my direction.

And then, to drive the point home that 'Salvation is of the Lord' (Jonah 2:9), I came to the latter part of chapters 8 to 11 of Romans. I was shattered. While my eyes had always been on what *I* had done with Jesus, the focus was now resting on what *Jesus* had done with me, before the creation of the world!

I did not know how to handle these discoveries. Oh, I knew that they were truths inspired by God; after all, they were right there in front of me as I turned the pages of Scripture. But it took a little longer to accept them. Passing from the stage of assent to that of consent is, of course, no small matter, especially when the subject under discussion is of such a revolutionary nature.

While beginning this journey, I came across a quotation from Jonathan Edwards, the leader of the Great Awakening in eighteenth-century America. I could identify with his testimony because it was so much a part of my own. He admitted that at first he responded in outrage — outrage that God would determine who would go to heaven. Then he was struck by fear; these ideas seemed unpleasant. After all, they emphasize the utter inability of the human will to choose God apart from God's own activity. However, Edwards finally burst into praise and worship of God as his bitterness turned into gratitude, as confusion turned into comfort.

We all naturally crave self-determination, and we like to think that we are ultimately in control of our future. Believing in the Lord of history is one thing; believing in the Lord of our future is quite another. God can count hairs and handle the sparrows, but when it comes to the specifics of *our* lives, we disapprove of God's sudden 'intrusion' into our destiny. We rebel at the idea of a salvation that is 'not of him who wills, nor of him who runs, but of God who shows mercy' (Rom. 9:16).

By the time I reached thirteen, I had completed the first draft of what is now this book. It was originally designed as a depository for my discoveries, a diary of the progression of my journey through Scripture. I now had a real reason for living, since I knew that God, the Creator of the universe, had a purpose for my life. I was part of a plan, a mission to be accomplished! God became real to me the more I perceived him as active instead of passive. I found greater harmony between God and me as my spiritual ego was being deflated (and continues to be, if ever so slowly) to make room for his glory. There were no more disappointing bouts of inspecting myself twenty-four hours a day to see if I was still keeping things going; nor was there any more patting myself on the back for something God did.

In some ways, most of us can identify with the crowd who heard Paul's sermon on Mars' Hill, as he 'stood . . . and said, "Men of Athens, I perceive that in all things you are very religious; for as I was passing through and considering the objects of your worship, I even found an altar with this inscription: To The Unknown God. Therefore, the One whom you worship without knowing, him I proclaim to you"' (Acts 17:22-23).

Paul goes on to describe the unknown God as the 'Lord of heaven and earth', the one who 'gives to all life, breath, and all things', the Governor who 'has determined [our] preappointed times . . . for in him we live and move and have our being'. This sermon was delivered from the heart of a man who was gripped by God's omnipotent grace.

The problem in Athens was not that people were not religious, God-fearing, zealous, pious worshippers; they simply did not know whom they were worshipping. No wonder that unbelievers are groping in the dark for a god to worship today, be it materialism, success, power, self, or religion. After all, many of us Christians are offering prayers, conducting services, performing religious acts and pious exercises for a God we do not even know.

Seeing myself as, first created in God's image, then fallen and in utter despair and helplessness and, finally, restored, has made me more able to look at my condition realistically. Now I can understand why I do what I do, and can know just what I am dealing with. I see myself as someone who has been selected out of a world of chaos, hopelessness and despair to be 'in Christ', as God's pre-selected child for all eternity.

Knowing that I am someone whom God has 'accepted in the Beloved' (Eph. 1:6) is a source of great comfort and security, especially in a world where acceptance and self-identity are based on performance. Then also, to know myself, I must see myself as redeemed, a rebel who has been fully reconciled to God. And how can a believer know himself or herself apart from understanding that he or she is a 'new creation' with a new identity?

In his autobiographical film, *Purple Rain,* Prince, a rock star of the mid-1980s says, 'I know times are changin'. We're reaching out for something new.' But, as the film attests, Prince cannot find anything new that is of any great substance. Times *are* changing, but God is always stable.

Many people in the world, including many Christians, are reaching out for something deeper, fuller and more profound. They want to see a heavenly Father who plans, acts and accomplishes, a Saviour who can actually save without needing human approval, a Holy Spirit who can bring us effectively into union with the living Christ — against all odds — and end this painful hostility between creature and Creator!

The ultimate questions people of our day are asking are these: 'What is the meaning of life? What is the purpose behind my life and my destiny?'

What questions are we evangelicals asking? Is dancing a sin? Should we baptize by immersion, sprinkling or pouring? Who is the next logical candidate for Antichrist? While we are busy at conferences and conventions, talking with ourselves about the need for Christian aerobics, or coming up with four new and painless steps to victorious Christian living, the world is taking its business elsewhere — to merchants who apply their philosophy to the deep, essential questions of human life. Philosopher Paul C. Payne noted, 'The world doesn't take the church seriously today because the church is not serious.'[2]

When we discover again that our faith has something meaningful to say to this world, and when we recognize that we as believers form 'a chosen race, a royal priesthood, a holy nation,' then we will once more see God at work in our needy world.

The more I understand the purpose behind my life, the more I am convinced of what the mission of the church on this planet is to be. The church is a new humanity, a new spiritual race. As a rib was taken from Adam's side to create a woman, so God has taken people 'out of every tribe and tongue and people and nation, and [has] made us kings and priests to our God' (Rev. 5:9).

This new race exists for a reason, a definite purpose. It exists to make God's glory and presence felt in a dark and drab world; the new race is to infiltrate all levels of society, in every nation, with the good news of God's saving grace. In short, the church is the outpost of the kingdom of God in this world. It is intended to be an island of certainty in a sea of despair.

If the church is to fulfil her mission in the world, we will have to return to the biblical gospel that clearly proclaims that salvation is the product of God, not man, nor God and man.

In my developing excitement over the biblical faith, I began searching through history for my spiritual roots. I discovered that, curiously, these truths and the world view they produced were the motivating force behind the greatest movements of the ages. It was more than coincidental that the periods of intense and vital witness were the times in which the fulness of the gospel was faithfully proclaimed. On the other hand, the periods of lethargy, compromise and lack of impact were the times when this message was silenced.

Columbia University history professor, Eugene F. Rice, Jr, says, 'All the more strikingly it [the Reformation doctrines of human inability and sovereign election] measures the gulf between the secular imagination of the twentieth century and sixteenth-century Protestantism's intoxication with the majesty of God. We can only exercise historical sympathy to try to understand how it was that many of the most sensitive intelligences of a whole epoch found a supreme, a total, liberty in the abandonment of human weakness to the omnipotence of God.'[3]

So what about the church today? What is the assessment as we make our way into the twenty-first century?

We find it far easier to nod as if we agree with someone than to explain why we don't. Many Christians today simply do not want to dig into significant doctrinal themes, especially at the risk of alienating those believers who disagree. I can understand that. We are tired of fighting, we have been through too many wars, too many anathemas and threatening shouts across the table. We need peace, unity and love, in spite of our diversity.

But, in quoting the prophet Jeremiah, Martin Luther wisely reminded us of the futility and, in fact, dishonesty, of crying, '"Peace, peace!" when there is no peace' (Jer. 6:14). Although we must be at peace, we cannot sit idly by to watch the doctrinal and theological content of our faith effervesce into oblivion. Truth is something our age scorns so cynically yet craves so passionately.

We prefer piety of practice to purity of faith. These doctrines have survived as some of the most significant themes of church history. 'But again, that's doctrine,' some reply, as if doctrine were by definition the opposite of what is truly important or useful. But, as Tyron Edwards remarked, 'Doctrine is the necessary foundation of duty; if the theory is not correct, the practice cannot be right. Tell me what a man believes, and I will tell you what he will do.' Even Ralph Waldo Emerson said, 'Pure doctrine always bears fruit in pure benefits.' Faith and practice are inseparably related.

Doctrine does not divide; it unites. A core of doctrine held that band of saints together as they faced martyrdom in the Roman Colosseum; doctrine brought both the peasant and the king together during the Reformation. Error divides, and since error is brought to greater visibility in the light of truth, often truth is blamed as the agent of division rather than error.

While on my journey, I have seen many people experience

what they half humorously and half seriously call 'being born again . . . again' — an encounter with a radical view of God and his relationship to them. I know myself well enough to be confident that nothing short of this message would have so captivated me since the age of thirteen. I am easily distracted, hopping from one hobby to another. Yet ever since I first discovered it the sovereign grace of God has preoccupied and excited my mind, heart and soul.

'Make your calling and election sure, for if you do these things you will never stumble' (2 Peter 1:10). 'You will never stumble'! At a time when the church has little interest in calling and election at all, no wonder she is stumbling in the dark. Here is an opportunity to get back on the track, a chance to see *your* life as a 'mission accomplished'!

2.
Created with class

Whenever we think of what God has done for us, the starting-point must be creation, not redemption. The cross must be understood in the context of other events. For until we begin to appreciate the glory of creation, the majesty of God's eternal purpose for us, the cross and the resurrection will not make a full impact on our lives.

The memory of creation

This is why Paul begins his epistle to the Romans by outlining the general revelation of God in creation. The glorious imprimatur of God's handiwork that surrounds us holds us responsible for accepting or rejecting God's reign over us.

'What happens to the heathen?' is a question often asked. Is there really a class of people who have *never* heard? 'For since the creation of the world his invisible attributes are clearly seen, being understood by the things that are made, even his eternal power and Godhead, so that they [the heathen] are without excuse' (Rom. 1:20).

There is no such person as an atheist. People do 'suppress the truth in unrighteousness' (Rom. 1:18), but you cannot suppress something that you do not believe exists. The creature will always remain the offspring and dependent of the Creator, whether the creature recognizes God in this life, or is judged by God in the next. Look, too, at the crucial role our conscience plays in this: 'For when Gentiles [heathen], who do not have the law, by nature do the things contained in the law, these, although not having the law, are a law to themselves, who show the work of the law written in their hearts, their conscience also bearing witness, and between themselves their thoughts accusing or else excusing them' (Rom. 2:14-15).

Have you ever recognized Jesus Christ as your Creator? We often talk about Jesus being our Saviour and Lord. But this message to the Romans reveals that Jesus Christ is recognized as Lord of creation: 'His invisible attributes are clearly seen . . . by the things that are made' (1:20). John said of Jesus, 'All things were made through him, and without him nothing was made' (John 1:3).

Four lessons from creation

1. Christ, Ruler of all life

'In the beginning *God . . .*' (Gen. 1:1). History and the record of divine revelation begins and ends with God. Time and space revolve round the one true God, known in three persons (the Trinity), by whose command every atom is governed. God establishes before anything else that he is the source of all that exists.

Jesus Christ is revealed in Scripture as the Creator of all life. Today we often recognize him as the ruler of our spiritual lives, but we somehow leave the secular realm to others. This lesson teaches us that we cannot make such distinctions as secular and spiritual. Let's look more closely at this point.

1. Jesus is the Lord of work. One look at the biblical accounts of creation will reveal that God takes work seriously. God does not look at a task and sigh, 'Just another day on the job.' There was nothing mediocre about God's creation. He saw each day of creation as a challenge to innovate, to build, to paint, to plant and to animate mud into a living person bearing his own image.

2. Jesus is the Lord of creativity. After all, that is what being a creator is all about. Because we have been created in God's image, we also possess the innate passion and capability to create. God looks at tasks and relationships as opportunities to be creative. Did you ever think about the fact that you are a co-creator with God? God looks at things that previously did not exist and says, 'Let there be . . .' That is God's attitude towards life. We can learn from that; though we are fallen, we are still created in the image of God.

3. Jesus is the Lord of the imagination. At a time when the images of the inner soul have been mortgaged for the images of the screen, imagination is lacking. When God wants to create something, he pictures it in his mind and commands, 'Let there be . . .' Of course, our creativity isn't in the same category as God's, when it comes to that, but the principle of creation is still there.

4. Jesus is the Lord of leisure. What on earth could leisure have to do with God? Plenty. God worked for six days. He rested on the seventh day and told us to take the day off, too. The volume of scriptural material related to God's interest in our free time leads us to obey his revealed will for the use of it and to thank him for the freedom to enjoy the gifts he has so graciously provided for those times. Did you have a good time last Friday night? Then thank God for it!

5. Jesus is the Lord of civilization. God called culture into being by building it upon the family — Adam and Eve. Not long afterwards families started building cities. Too often we Christians see culture and society as being 'out there', not part of our concern. When George Orwell talks about 'Big Brother', or philosophers decry and debate the fall of Western civilization, so many of us in the evangelical community respond, 'So what?' After all, Jesus said things would get worse and worse and then he would come and take us away from this mess, didn't he?

Regardless of your view of the end times, the cultural mandate — the precedent established by God in Eden to build a civilization, populate the earth, subdue it, tame it and bring it under the moral absolutes of divine revelation — is still in effect. You and I are still responsible to create, to use our imagination, to enjoy life and the total range of human activity, to work and to build a better civilization.

We could discuss other areas in which Jesus Christ, as the

second person of the Holy Trinity, is Lord. He expects us to use and enjoy his gifts of food and drink, friendships (and not just with other Christians), athletics, music and the arts. There is no such thing as secular music; there are no secular sports; we search in vain to find secular friendships or secular food and drink. All that is not expressly evil is created by God for our benefit and his glory.

We are called to live in the light of creation. We are invited to be reconciled to the one in whose image we were created. Let us look at the Scriptures to get a better grasp of our created image so that we will understand our creativity — our sense of purpose, dignity and worth — and our sense of awe at our significance in this massive universe.

2. Christ makes order out of chaos

Before God created it, 'The earth was without form, and void; and darkness was on the face of the deep. And the Spirit of God was hovering over the face of the waters' (Gen. 1:2).

The second lesson the creation teaches us is that God creates things *ex nihilo,* 'from nothing'.

We finite creatures can know life only in terms of causes and effects. I might paint a picture; but I have paint, a canvas and some brushes with which to work. It is unreasonable to us that something should come from nothing. 'If God created the world, who created God?' many of us ask. But God is the first cause of all that is. In the beginning we have God, staring as it were into an incalculable abyss of empty space. After six days, God has created order!

We need to keep this image in mind as we examine the doctrines of salvation: God creates something from nothing; he brings order out of chaos. The further apart we are from God, the more chaotic our lives will be. Reconciled to God, we have harmony and order. What did creation possess of its own before it existed? Darkness, formlessness, lack of shape and purpose, void and emptiness. These words are a perfect description of our lives when lived apart from God.

3. Christ acts on purpose and is not at the mercy of events

The third lesson we learn from creation is that God governs

the universe. Nothing happens at random. Randomness is simply not God's way; nor does it show up in the reality of this world. Historians can chart the course of world events to the present. Chemists can describe a pattern for the universe. All it would take would be one atom to upset the make-up of one molecule. To take it to its logical conclusion, we could foresee a hopeless situation if the universe were operating at random.

In his best seller *When Bad Things Happen to Good People,* Harold Kushner states, 'Bad things do happen to good people in this world, but it is not God who wills it. God would like people to get what they deserve in life, but he cannot always arrange it. Even God has a hard time keeping chaos in check and limiting the damage evil can do.'[1]

Such a limited view of God is rooted in a basic misunderstanding of the Creator as revealed in the creation, not to mention in a weak view of the Fall.

Kushner seems to say that the universe has two gods, two equally powerful sources: God the Creator and Chaos. Thus by chapter 3 (which is called, 'Sometimes there is no reason'), Kushner asserts that 'There is randomness in the universe.' 'Why,' he asks, 'do we have to insist on everything being reasonable? Why can't we let the universe have a few rough edges?'[2]

The answer to these questions is that our God is a God of purpose and everything happens for a specific reason because God does not waste time on meaningless, random events. Why can we say that? Look at the details of creation. The psalmist said that God 'counts the number of the stars; he calls them all by name' (Ps. 147:4).

God even sees to it that the spots on a bird's feathers form a pattern. He demonstrates the same concern for the details of the pattern in our lives.

God is both Creator and Lord of creation, and chance, fate, or randomness simply do not exist. One random event — no matter how inherently insignificant — could be the missing link that held together an entire chain! We can have confidence in the future because we know God has been in charge of our past.

Another way to say this is to say that God does everything on purpose. God is intentional in everything he does. Human governments and heads of state are often surprised by developments and events that take place, seeing them as unexpected complexities. But nothing is complex or surprising to God.

Perhaps one reason why men and women either grope for meaning and purpose or give up on the existence of meaning and purpose altogether is that they no longer believe that God has a purpose. We have gone beyond questioning the idea whether there is any order or design in the universe at all. We see this in the rejection of absolutes ('This is definitely right' and 'This is positively wrong') in theology, morality, politics, art, and so on.

We need to come back to 'In the beginning God created the heavens and the earth.' Because God created us with purpose and with meaning, we can live purposefully, knowing that our life counts towards something significant — the glory of God. As José Luis Martin Descalzo said, 'If *God* is lacking, nothing a man does is of any more consequence than the acts of a mouse.'

4. Christ makes us significant

The fourth lesson from creation teaches the inspiring truth that we are significant.

Satellite dishes are launched into space to be open eyes to the cosmos, begging the discovery of something or someone truly significant, someone to reveal what really counts in this universe. Earth cannot give us meaning. The structures of earth make us feel small and insignificant. Often we are walked on, climbed over, beaten down, and put down in this hurry-up-and-get-it-done-yesterday world.

Modern science, with all its elaborate and in many cases enlightening analyses, has failed to come up with any basis for human value or significance.

Sir John Eccles, Nobel laureate and a pioneer in brain research, says, 'The law of gravitation was not the final truth,' going on to explain how many modern scientists have turned the discipline into a 'superstition' by claiming that 'We only have to know more about the brain' to understand ourselves and our significance. Eccles concludes: 'Science cannot explain the existence of each of us as a unique self, nor can it answer such fundamental questions as: Who am I? Why am

I here? How did I come to be at a certain place and time? What happens after death? These are all mysteries beyond science.'[3]

Notice Eccles's indictment of modern science: 'Science has gone too far in breaking down man's belief in his spiritual greatness and has given him the belief that he is merely an insignificant animal who has arisen by chance and necessity on an insignificant planet lost in the great cosmic immensity.'[4]

Much of science has turned away from divine revelation and, therefore, from God. Consequently, our uniqueness, our significance in this universe is based on whatever the microscope or the telescope can probe and what cause-and-effect events the technician can monitor. The doctrine of creation, as revealed in Scripture, turns our attention back to the Creator, showing us that someone of infinite significance has created us as key figures in the universe.

While the secularists look to themselves for significance only to discover how small and finite they are, believers can look to God and discover their immortality. This revelation lifts persons out of the animal kingdom and attaches great significance to their temporal and eternal existence.

The secularist philosophers have tried their hand at it, too. They tell us, as theologian R. C. Sproul puts it, 'We emerged from insignificance; our destiny is insignificant, but somehow, in between all of this insignificance, we're significant!' The doctrine of creation teaches us that our origin is significant because our originator is the standard of significance. French philosopher Henri Frederic Amiel said, 'I realize with intensity that man, in all he does that is great and noble, is only the organ of something or someone higher than himself.'

What makes a man noble and great is the fact that his Author is great and noble, and that humanity was the only species of creation to be made in the image of God, to be created in the image of nobility and greatness!

British philosopher Philip James Bailey said, 'Let each man think himself an act of God.' What a bold pronouncement! And yet that is precisely what we are. As God is the basis for all human value and significance, rejecting the centrality of God in the universe strips us of any claim to fame. In such a case, maybe the dead-end philosophers are right. Perhaps we *are* just a cosmic belch that will soon diffuse into the atmosphere, to make way for some other incidental, random accident to come along.

We must, therefore, preach the sovereign purpose of God in creation (our origin) as well as in divine election (our destiny). We must remind the world that we are all here for a reason and that our origin insists upon our significance.

The purpose of it all

Every craft points to the skill and nature of the craftsman. And creation speaks eloquently of its Creator. Now that we have seen that creation has a purpose, let's find out what that purpose is.

A popular theory says that God created humans because God was lonely. I call this the Lone Ranger theory. Augustine would have been surprised that believers should come up with this theory. He once said, 'In every man there is a God-shaped vacuum that only he can fill.' The Lone Ranger theory, on the other hand, says, 'In God there is a human-shaped vacuum that only humans can fill.'

The difference here is much more than a semantic shift in emphasis. Instead the basic strategy is changed, making creation human-centred rather than God-centred. God was never lonely. The dictionary defines *'loneliness'* as 'the absence of company, as being 'destitute of sympathetic companionship'. One would hardly think that the Holy Trinity amid the hosts of heaven would constitute an abyss of loneliness! God is not lonely without men and women. Are we seriously suggesting that God was lacking something all through the aeons of eternity before our creation? Rather we are lonely without God.

Well, if God did not create us because he was lonely, why did he create us?

The Scriptures outline the purpose of creation as the supreme stage on which God has chosen to act out the drama of his glory, goodness, justice and power. The psalmist's prayer tells the story:

'O Lord, how manifold are your works!
In wisdom you have made them all.
The earth is full of your possessions —

This great and wide sea,
In which are innumerable teeming things,
Living things both small and great . . .
What you give them they gather in;
You open your hand, they are filled with good.
You hide your face, they are troubled;
You take away their breath, they die and
    return to their dust.
You send forth your Spirit,
    they are created;
And you renew the face of the earth.
May the glory of the Lord endure for ever;
May the Lord rejoice in his works'

(Ps. 104:24-25, 28-31).

You see, similar to 'Why did God create us?' is the question, 'Why do potters make pots?' Making pots is what a potter *does*; that is a potter's identity. And good potters are known for their work. Why did Da Vinci paint the *Mona Lisa*? He painted because he was an artist, with the urge to create, and saw the piece as a challenge to create. God is the greatest creator of all. Therefore, we would expect God to create — and to create the finest.

Creation is certainly a mystery — shades of 'how?', 'why?', and 'what if . . .' But we can be secure and content in knowing that we are here on earth for the purpose of 'glorifying God and enjoying him for ever' (Westminster Shorter Catechism). That is reason enough!

The word is out

While those satellite dishes beg a response from someone important out there in the universe, the Author of the universe has in fact already spoken. The first words God spoke that are recorded in Scripture are: 'Let there be light.' God's word has the power to create. The psalmist recorded, 'By the word of the Lord the heavens were made, and all the host of them by the breath of his mouth' (Ps. 33:6).

A popular securities firm boasts that when it talks, people listen. But when God talks, people not only listen, but things happen! When we wake up in the morning to the sunlight, we are reminded again of the eternal power of God's Word. The darkness, emptiness and void simply were no match for God's word. Light invaded darkness and brought beauty to a blank canvas.

In the Gospel of John we read a parallel passage to this first chapter of Genesis. Although we will look more closely at its implications later in this book, it may help at this point to recognize the identity of this 'Word' of God: 'In the beginning was the Word, and the Word was with God, and the Word was God. He was in the beginning with God. All things were made through him, and without him nothing was made that was made. In him was life, and the life was the light of men. And the light shines in the darkness, and the darkness did not comprehend it' (John 1:1-5).

This 'Word' is, of course, God the Son. The same light that invaded the darkness of pre-creation still invades the darkness of our lives today. God has spoken, God has created and has placed us within two book-ends of history.

Indeed, we have been created with class!

3.
Rebels without a cause

Like many other children, I tried my hand at making and selling lemonade when I was a boy. I can recall my thriving enterprise at the roadside. I spent more time mixing the lemonade than actually selling it. It was never enough for me just to follow the instructions on the label of the can. No, I had to add my own unique ingredients.

I have to admit in all honesty that the lemonade tasted a great deal better before my additions. Even though I knew deep down that instead of improving the flavour I was actually polluting it, the pride of simply knowing that I had something to do with the final product became more important to me than the quality of the product.

How often have we encountered the 'lemonade phenomenon' in everyday life! The advertisers keep telling us to 'have it your way,' and we really like that. At the heart of the 'lemonade phenomenon' in the matter of our relationship with God is our failure to recognize the seriousness of what happens when we do things our way.

The early returns are in

When God had surveyed his new creation, he said, 'It is good.' Nature was good, the land and the seas were good, and the air was good. Most importantly, man and woman were good.

God was never distant. Adam and Eve often conversed with God. 'Then the Lord God took the man and put him in the garden of Eden to tend and keep it. And the Lord God commanded the man, saying, "Of every tree of the garden you may freely eat; but of the tree of the knowledge of good and evil you shall not eat, for in the day that you eat of it you shall surely die." And the Lord God said, "It is not good that man should be alone; I will make him a helper comparable to him'" (Gen. 2:15-18).

You know the story. They sinned and they were ashamed. The narrative goes on to report Adam and Eve's attempt, not only to cover themselves with fig leaves, but to run from God's presence. Then God sentenced all creation for the rebellion of the one who was created in his image.

Notice the process involved in Adam's fatal decision. It began with Satan's direct rebellion against God's word: 'You will *not* surely die' (Gen. 3:4). There was no beating about the bush here. Satan always plays down the gravity of sin. What he was really saying was this: 'Look, Eve, you're not looking at this with an open mind. The first thing you have to realize is that this "punishment" that God is hanging over your head really isn't as bad as it sounds. As with the rest of us, God's bark is worse than his bite.'

The clincher comes when Satan appeals to the instinct that led to his own rebellion: pride. Here is where human beings take the bait: 'You will be like God' (Gen. 3:5). And we have been taking the bait ever since. 'Invictus,' a nineteenth-century poem by William Ernest Henley, expresses well our urge to be our own god:

> I thank whatever gods that be
> For my unconquerable soul.
>
> I am the master of my fate:
> I am the captain of my soul.

Adam's problem was that he agreed with Satan's arrogant claim that he actually could be independent of his Creator. Adam's attitude of complete dependence and surrender to God was now turned into an explosion of insulted pride. Adam and Eve could believe that God was suppressing them. 'Maybe I *do* have an unconquerable soul,' they began to reason. I can even imagine Eve's saying, 'Well, I've got to be myself.'

Let's look a little closer at this idea of independence and try to understand why this animosity between the Creator and ourselves still exists.

We cannot have absolute justice (decisions that we can say conclusively are right) unless we have an absolute Judge.

We cannot have absolute beauty unless we have an absolute Creator. Artists, for example, sometimes paint pictures of nature: a field of buttercups, a landscape, ordinary people performing ordinary tasks. What person with normal vision would say of a peacock, 'That's an ugly bird'? We once believed that our Creator designed things with so much skill that one could paint a picture of those things and *know* that the representation would be beautiful. Today, the popular artist looks to his inner self for psychoanalysis as the subject of his paintings. What is beautiful to one person is repulsive to another. We can't be sure how creative we are ever since we lost our Creator.

We cannot have law and order unless we have an absolute Law-giver and Orderer.

We cannot have absolute knowledge unless there is one who absolutely knows — and who decides to share his knowledge with us.

The truth of the matter is that we need God a great deal more than he needs us; in fact, God doesn't need us at all. Since we were *created* in God's image, we become more human when we are *conformed* to God's image (see Rom. 8:29). Seeking fulfilment and self-expression in any other way is most unrealistic and ultimately proves fatal.

Our declaration of independence

In an essay titled, 'What Really Matters?' *Time* magazine sought to define 'the idea characterizing [our] age'. The article suggested that the twentieth-century spirit was distinguished by its determination to break away from traditional norms 'and eventually from any constraints at all'. Furthermore, 'Behind most of these events lay the assumption that what was not free *ought* to be free; that limits were intrinsically evil.'

Time's provocative critique of modern culture draws its

conclusion about 'our age of self-confident autonomy' by noting, 'When people are unfettered they are freed, but not yet free.'[1] This reporter understood more than Adam and Eve understood that day when they gave in to Satan's grandiose notion of 'self-confident autonomy'. Yet, it is precisely that notion that has kept God and humans apart since the Fall in Eden. Adam and Eve resented God. 'How dare God with-hold from us the knowledge of good and evil?' they asked.

It is interesting that the vogue, *avant-garde,* 'in' thing today is the knowledge of good and evil — in fact, to the point where the lines separating the two regions disappear altogether. We talk about the modern sexual revolution, for instance. But the movement is about as modern as the Garden of Eden itself. Remember, Satan promised, 'Your eyes will be opened' (Gen. 3:5). Adam and Eve were 'enlightened', to be sure. But was that worth the condemnation of creation?

I found the following lines written on a painting in a small cafe:

> I have taken the pill.
> I have hoisted my skirts to my thighs,
> Dropped them to my ankles,
> Rebelled at the university,
> Skied at Aspen,
> Lived with two men,
> Married one,
> Earned my keep,
> Kept my identity,
> And frankly . . .
> I'm lost.

Ours is indeed a generation that has seen it all. Many teen-agers are experienced in sex, drugs and life in general. Men boast about their 'macho' infidelity to their wives, and women rebel against their role in the created order. A generation on the rampage for 'finding itself' is losing hope in there being any real resolution to the questions, 'Who am I?' or, 'Why am I here?'

The tragedy of the Fall is seen in contrast to the glory of cre-ation. When I was younger, I fell and broke my arm. The first question my mother asked was, 'How high were you?' Had I been two steps up the ladder, she would not have worried so much. But I was on the roof; that presented a much more dangerous image.

So, too, the fall of mankind takes on proportionately greater significance when we realize the height from which we have fallen. We were created to be God's eternal dependents. When Adam rejected that order, he upset the balance of the entire creation. The irony is that we are still dependent on the Creator, whether or not we admit it. 'For in him we live and move and have our being' (Acts 17:28). Just because Adam declared his independence did not mean that he actually achieved it.

Our fall was complete. Every area of human life was affected. Nothing created by God on earth was left untouched by this event. So the stain of sin touches us physically, emotionally, psychologically, mentally, morally and spiritually. Not long ago I was lamenting the fact that I thought one of my friends was neurotic. But the more I began to think about it, the more I realized that we are all neurotic to some degree! Total depravity does not mean that we are all nasty savages, although the potential is there. It means that the effects of the Fall are total. The cancer has spread into every part of the human condition.

The things we take for granted as being normal are distortions and contortions of a twisted world gone haywire. God created order out of chaos, and men and women have been trying ever since to undo that order. When our relationship with God was disrupted and diplomatic relations were, in a sense, broken off, all of life went wrong, not just our religious or devotional life.

Adam and Eve lost their identity. They knew that they had been created in the image of God, but they were not quite sure what they were now. They began to experience illnesses from time to time. They knew what it was to be fatigued and frustrated. They began to grow discontented with each other; in fact, it only took the second male, Adam's son, to murder his brother.

Guilt invaded innocence. Adam and Eve were now ashamed of their bodies — bodies that would soon decay and eventually die. They were disillusioned. Early in the story, they realized that trying to live their lives apart from God was essentially a denial of who they were (images of God). The image rejected the one whose reflection it was. Our first parents covered themselves with fig leaves. They wanted to work out their problems on their own. But their guilt was more than fig leaves could handle.

We need to stop running from God. We cannot find God for the same reason that a thief cannot find a policeman. If God catches up with us, he will expose our nakedness and insecurity. That is why Paul repeated the words of the psalmist when he lamented, 'There is none who understands, there is none who seeks after God' (Rom. 3:11).

What fig leaves are we wearing? God is not impressed with our empty offerings of human achievement. All have robbed God and there are no 'good' robbers or 'bad' robbers. The thief and the theologian must come to God on the same terms.

Our hope is in God's mercy. 'For the Son of Man has come to save that which was lost' (Matt. 18:11). Christ said, 'It is not those who are healthy who need a physician, but those who are ill . . . For I did not come to call the righteous, but sinners' (Matt. 9:12-13, NASB).

To put it simply, the first step to qualify for God's grace is to realize that you cannot qualify! After Christ brought his disciples to the place where they despaired of their efforts before God, they asked, 'Who then can be saved?'

He responded, 'With men this is impossible, but with God all things are possible' (Matt. 19:25-26).

Who is to blame?

Humans always look for a scapegoat. When confronted by God after his disobedience, Adam said in effect, 'It's *her* fault — the woman *you* gave me made me eat the fruit.' And Eve said, 'The devil made me do it.'

Precisely because our unbelieving world does not understand (or know about) the Fall, it is baffled by the cause and purpose of suffering, evil, and so on. As I mentioned in the last chapter, Harold Kushner gives us the alternative of choosing either a God who is good, or a God who is powerful. If bad things happen to good people, then either God is not good or God is not powerful enough to stop it. Kushner opts for the latter.

But the problem is not with God. The issue does not involve interrogating our Creator about his goodness or sovereignty, but rather looking in the mirror, because we are the cause of whatever is wrong in this world. When God took a look at what he had done, he said, 'It is good.' Our pride, arrogance and rebelliousness are only underlined by blaming God for, say, a bad environment while we continue to release our toxic, unnatural refuse in the air. But that is our way: we pollute life and then blame God for the results.

The problem is not with God at all — it never is. We have rebelled against our Creator and his design for the universe. The Fall reverses the act of creation by making chaos and confusion out of order. Blaming God for the results is simply unfair and unrealistic.

Although we are entirely responsible for our guilt, the Fall did not surprise God; in fact, it was a part of his plan. Romans 8:20-22, as well as many other passages, makes that clear: 'For the creation was subjected to futility, not willingly, but because of him who subjected it in hope; because the creation itself also will be delivered from the bondage of corruption into the glorious liberty of the children of God. For we know that the whole creation groans and labours with birth pangs together until now.'

Even when bad things happen to us, we know that God has a plan for them.

Lethal injection

We hear a lot today about AIDS, a deadly disease that is communicated, among other means, through blood transfusions. If someone with AIDS donates blood, and the blood is transfused into a patient's veins, the patient will probably get the disease.

When Adam turned against God, his nature was changed; and we inherit that fallen nature. All of Adam's children have received bad blood. Theologians call this concept 'original sin'. When Thomas Jefferson drafted the Declaration of Independence, he spoke for Americans living today. We were not actually there. However, this document represented us just the same as if we had been. And whenever a baby is born in the United States, that baby automatically becomes an American citizen and so is included in that Declaration of Independence. When that baby grows up, he or she will realize that representatives in government speak in his or her place on international and domestic issues.

Adam was our representative before God. He spoke in our place. As Adam's children, our nature is in complete harmony with his fallen nature. When we are born into Adam's race, we automatically assume Adamic citizenship and so are included in his declaration of independence. The psalmist confessed, 'In sin my mother *conceived* me' (Ps. 51:5). And Isaiah recognized that we are all 'rebel[s] from birth' (Isa. 48:8, NASB). Again, David said that we are 'estranged from the womb . . . [and] go astray from birth' (Ps. 58:3, NASB).

When a corporation dumps toxic chemicals into one end of a stream, that one area is not the only part of the stream affected. Pretty soon the pollution washes all the way down the stream, and the entire river is polluted. Adam's rebellion did not just affect his condition; our whole race was polluted — so much so that it has become useless before God: 'Together, they have become useless' (Rom. 3:12 NASB). One person is no better than another. We are all in this together.

When we are born, then, we are already at odds with the God for whose pleasure we were created. We are born in a war zone, not a neutral zone. And we are on the wrong side of the front! The problems we all face in ourselves, in each other and in the world, are ultimately rooted in our nature as fallen, alienated rebels. Humans do not merely do evil; they are evil. 'The heart is . . . desperately wicked; who can know it?' (Jer. 17:9). We not only fall; we are fallen. We not only get lost; we are lost.

While it is true that Adam was our representative and that we are heirs of his estrangement from God, we are personally responsible for our acts of unbelief and disobedience against God. Being 'by nature children of wrath' (Eph. 2:3) does not rule out our personal choices to turn from God. Someone has wisely noted that we are first, 'sinners by birth, and then sinners by choice'.

It helps us to know *why* we disobey God and turn from him,

but we are none the less guilty before God on our own merit. If you are not a believer, why are you not? Because *you* have decided not to be. That is your decision. That is everyone's decision apart from the grace of God. Nobody will be sentenced to eternal judgement simply because he or she inherited Adam's nature; all men and women will be judged also on the basis of their own evil acts. We each express our evil nature in our own unique way, according to the direction of our fallen will.

As a final note to our focus on ancestral and personal sin, let's recognize that we are not the victims of sin, but the cause and source of it. Of his own free will, Adam sinned and enslaved the will of humanity to sin. When we sin, it is our choice. And when we refuse to acknowledge God's authority over our lives, that is our choice. For that choice God will hold us accountable.

From bad to worse

The bad news only gets worse: 'Through one man sin entered the world, and death through sin, and thus death spread to all men, because all sinned . . . For . . . by the one man's offence many died' (Rom. 5:12, 15).

When we were born into this world, we were physically alive. We could respond to our world in a rather direct way — by crying. Yet, even in the presence of such demonstrations of physical life, we were spiritually stillborn. We did not and could not respond to the spiritual world as we did and could to the natural world.

God created man a living spirit. That is what makes us fully human. But God also warned that in the day Adam disobeyed him, he would surely die. Obviously, Adam did not die physically until many years later, but his spirit died that day. That spirit was really the only thing of substance that God had in common with his creation. So when Adam died spiritually, he lost all harmony with his Creator.

Ephesians 2:1 reads, 'You . . . were dead in trespasses and sins.' Statements of this kind appear throughout Scripture, emphasizing the tragic reality of our being cut off and severed from divine life.

Death carries with it the connotation of finality. When someone dies, we do not usually expect anything more to come from that person. If we call him or her by name, no matter how loudly, we receive no answer. To say that someone is dead is to say that he or she is unresponsive. That means that you and I do not communicate with God in the spiritual realm at all, unless we are somehow made alive by God. After all, 'The natural man does not receive the things of the Spirit of God, for they are foolishness to him; nor can he know them, because they are spiritually discerned' (1 Cor. 2:14).

In the Garden of Eden, then, did God pull the sheet up over the lifeless corpse of mankind? Was it all over for our race?

What can we do about all this?

We can do only what God gives us grace to do. That is the whole point of the gospel message: 'Salvation is of the Lord' (Jonah 2:9).

Something in all of us knows that we are at odds with God, that something is wrong. Adam and Eve demonstrated their fear by running from God, illustrating how we not only are not inclined to seek God, but we naturally choose to run in the other direction. But the point is that we know that something is wrong.

In a certain sense, many believers desire to have the account settled — on their own terms. But, if they admit they are helpless, they also have to conclude that they cannot call upon the name of the Lord without owing him their lives. People will very often say, 'I won't ask her for help; that will mean I owe her a favour.'

The more we admit needs to be done by God because of our helplessness, the more indebted we feel to God. And nobody likes to be in debt. We take a lot of pride in saying, 'I did it all on my own.' But the fact of the matter is that in spiritual matters, we can do nothing on our own.

One thing that the Scripture makes absolutely clear is that we depend entirely on God, not only for air, food and shelter, but also for salvation. Remember the confusion that resulted when people began building the Tower of Babel, hoping to reach God? We should have learned our lesson about building towers. God is out of our reach, but we are never out of his reach.

Suppose today's newspaper advertised a race to the planet Jupiter between a helicopter, a 747 and a Concorde jet. Which do you think would win? The helicopter is in the same boat with the Concorde because none of the aircraft will make it to Jupiter. Jupiter is in a different atmosphere entirely. Likewise, heaven is beyond everybody's reach. What difference does it make if you do the best you can when God isn't even watching?

God doesn't give marks for effort!

We can merit the favour of other people. For instance, many non-Christians are benevolent. A millionaire can make a large donation to charity, but as long as he is 'dead in trespasses and sins,' 'in Adam,' and a 'rebel by birth,' his generosity impresses only other people. 'Without faith it is impossible to please [God]' (Heb. 11:6). Seeking the favour of other people does not accomplish anything of eternal significance. But if we have the favour of God, everything we do takes on eternal value.

The whole point is that God must *bestow* on us his own merit if we are to receive his favour.

4.
It's God's move

'Be even more diligent to make your calling and election sure, for if you do these things you will never stumble' (2 Peter 1:10).

The doctrine of the Fall never has been popular, and we are encouraged to find that the Bible has another chapter. This story could have ended with God's judgement. Perhaps that is what the angels were fearing; certainly Satan thought he had finally ruined God's plans for the universe. In actual fact, Satan was only fulfilling them. The devil forgot to take account of God's love and mercy. Who thought God would set out to recover a race of rebels?

God never intended that the world should be left hanging out to dry. All along, he had a plan of rescue that was ready to be implemented at the proper time. Even when it appears there is no way out, God steps into the picture of despair and creates.

Every four years Americans go to the polls to choose a president. In an election, of course, we make a choice of one candidate from a larger field. The election separates the one chosen from all others. This same dynamic is seen in Christ's statement: 'I chose you out of the world' (John 15:19). But whereas we try to choose our leaders by their past record, Christ chooses us unconditionally. Jesus said, 'You did not choose me, but I chose you and appointed you that you should go and bear fruit, and that your fruit should remain' (John 15:16).

God has selected from this race of fallen rebels men, women and children to form an alternative race, a new spiritual humanity. Peter put it this way: 'You are a chosen race, a royal priesthood, a holy nation, a people for God's own possession' (1 Peter 2:9, NASB). One anonymous writer expressed his response this way:

> 'Tis not that I did choose thee,
> For Lord, that could not be;
> This heart would still refuse thee,
> Hadst thou not chosen me.

The writer of that hymn was convinced of an inability to achieve salvation. The author knew that his or her condition, apart from God's intervention, was so critical that he or she would never have chosen God unless God had chosen him or her first.

We would still be running from God, trying to cover up our guilt on our own if God had not determined to make us his own possession. If we are to become God's children, it will be because he, 'in love ... predestined us to adoption as sons' (Eph. 1:5). The consuming nature of sin and the finality of its results, therefore, call for a decisive move on God's part if anyone is to be saved.

Remember, our identity is either 'in Adam' or 'in Christ'. Ephesians 1:4 informs us that 'He [the Father] chose us in him [the Son] ..., that we should be holy and without blame before him.' Because of God's choosing, then, our identity is transferred from the frailty of Adam to the family of God.

But I object!

Why is the subject of election or predestination so divisive? Why is it that whenever the terms are brought up, people move to other parts of the room? I'll tell you what, if you ever want a sure way to get rid of unwanted guests just ask them about election or predestination! I guarantee they will hit the road! To be sure, most of the passages addressed in this book are not the ones underlined in most believers' Bibles. Why is this?

D. James Kennedy suggests, 'The reason people today are opposed to it is because they will have God to be anything but God. He can be a cosmic psychiatrist, a helpful shepherd, a leader, a teacher, anything at all ... only not God. For a very simple reason — they want to be God themselves.'[1]

You see, we can talk about grace, sing about grace, preach about grace, just so long as we do not get too close to it. For if we do, we will be led irreversibly to election.

Let's examine some of the questions raised in connection with this teaching.

1. 'Doesn't election deny free will? If God has already made my decision for me, I really don't have any choice in the matter.'

Sometimes a person does not have a choice in certain areas of life. A prisoner, for example, has no control over whether the governor will grant a pardon. The decision is out of the prisoner's hands. Similarly, what choices can someone who is dead in trespasses and sins make concerning a relationship to God? He or she needs a pardon from the Governor of the universe.

Our nature is not to respond to God. If left to ourselves, no persuasion, no technique will ever change our basic character of independence and rejection of the authority of God. God must intervene. We do not choose God in our natural state — not just because we cannot do so, but also because we *will not*. That is the pitiful, yet realistic view of our condition. We are blind and out of touch with the eternal and divine. Our hearts are hard.

Essentially, what election is about is God's making for us the decision that we would never have made left to ourselves. We had our backs turned to God, yet God turned us round and determined to give us life again. 'In this is love, not that we loved God, but that he loved us' (1 John 4:10).

'Whosoever will, let him come!' — that is the unqualified call of Scripture. If anyone does 'will' to come, it is because he or she has been converted by God's grace. Hence, when someone does choose Christ, as far as the person is concerned, it is a free choice. Because God has changed our natural disposition from being against him, to one that is for him, we now make the decision that is in harmony with our new, converted nature.

Paul announced that salvation is 'not of him who wills, nor

of him who runs, but of God who shows mercy' (Rom. 9:16). That does not mean that we do not will, nor that we do not run; but it does mean that salvation ultimately depends on the will, decision and work of God, and not on us. Perhaps that is at first insulting, but it is certainly better than the alternative.

2. *'Election is deterministic. It is a salvation of fate, not love.'*

Unless you believe that the universe has no purpose, order, or design at all, you are a determinist. Either you believe that God has determined history, or that human beings determine it. God 'works all things according to the counsel of his will' (Eph. 1:1). We should be relieved that God determines history. I would hate to think that my affairs were left to chance, or to what other people determined for me. It comforts me to know that my earthly and heavenly destiny is in God's hands.

Even though election necessarily says, 'Yes, salvation is pre-determined,' it is the arch-enemy of the error of fatalism. If God merely provided salvation for everybody, then stepped back to see where the chips fell, that would indeed be fatalism, as summed up in the saying: 'Whatever will be, will be.'

But this is not the case. Christ says, 'I know my sheep' (John 10:14). Our salvation is not in the hands of fate, but in the hands of a loving and just heavenly Father. Love, not fate, is the basis of election. 'In love he predestined us' (Eph. 1:5, NASB). Romans 8:29 teaches: 'For whom he foreknew, he also predestined.' This verse teaches us that salvation is based on God's initiating love, a love that reaches us from right back in eternity past.

3. *'Election is unfair. How can God tell people, "Sorry, but you're just not on the list"?'*

Perhaps you remember when Joseph's brothers sold him into slavery out of jealousy. Through God's providence, Joseph eventually became the prime minister of Egypt and, when his brothers came to him during the famine, he revealed his identity and gave them Egypt's finest land, goods and services. The brothers were, of course, surprised at Joseph's kindness in the light of what they had done.

What if Joseph had just given two of his brothers the gifts? We would have been surprised if he had given each one of them gifts after what they had done to him. They deserved judgement, but instead were given gifts.

I believe that the accusation of injustice in God for choosing one person and not another is rooted in the fact that we have really lost our doctrine of grace today. We no longer really believe that nobody deserves salvation. We no longer really believe in grace. If we did believe that people were saved in spite of the fact that they deserve the opposite, we would accept election as a logical (as well as a scriptural) conclusion. Paul could not separate election and grace in his mind. In fact, he called the doctrine 'the election of grace' (Rom. 11:5). What is fair? Surely it is getting what we deserve. But can you name one person who deserves God?

I used to have a problem with election, even when I was confronted with it in the Scriptures. The crux of my problem was that I could not understand why God should have chosen *me*. Why not my next-door neighbour? I struggled at length with that question. I have come to the conclusion that my reluctance was rooted in some basic misunderstanding.

My first misunderstanding was in what election is. Election does not exclude anybody from the kingdom of God. That is the wrong emphasis. Rather, election includes those whose direction is away from the kingdom of God and who would otherwise remain for ever in the kingdom of sin and death.

Secondly, I misunderstood the gravity of my sin. I finally saw that if God was going to give us all what we deserve, we would all end up in the lake of fire. We do not ask a philanthropic millionaire why he helps one person and not another. After all, it is his money. The millionaire is not under any obligation to help anybody. Neither is God.

Thirdly, I misunderstood the nature of God. God is holy. His character demands punishment for sin. That is because he is just. God's mercy is never expected; therefore, if even one sinner is chosen by God, it is a big surprise. God is also free: he doesn't have to choose anybody at all!

The Scriptures give many examples of God's freedom in his selective grace. Near a pool in Jerusalem gathered 'a great multitude of sick people, blind, lame, paralysed' (John 5:3). Yet Christ pushed through the crowd and moved towards one man — just one person — and healed him from his paralysis. Why didn't he heal everybody who was sick at the pool that day? Did he have the power to do so? He created them, so we can assume that he had the power to restore them. We may only answer, 'It was not in his plan.' That is all we need to know.

Instead of calling God 'unfair' for not healing everybody, instead we praise him for the life he did restore. It should be no different when we speak about God's plan for the healing of people's hearts and souls.

William Shakespeare said, 'That word "grace" on the lips of an ungrateful person is profane.' Those were strong words, but I think that it is time that we began to see grace for what it is: undeserved favour. If we were truly grateful and truly believed in grace, we would be writing hymns of praise to God for electing so many thousands of rebels, rather than insulting his generosity by asking, 'Why didn't you choose everybody?'

The famous nineteenth-century evangelist Charles Spurgeon said, 'What amazes me is not that God does not choose everybody, but rather that he chose *me*.' He also saw election as an area outside the realm of human justification and prayed once, 'Lord, save the elect, then elect some more.'

The apostle Paul wrote, 'So then he has mercy on whom he desires, and he hardens whom he desires. You will say to me then, "Why does he still find fault? For who resists his will?" On the contrary, who are you, O man, who answers back to God? The thing moulded will not say to the moulder, "Why did you make me like this," will it? Or does not the potter have a right over the clay, to make from the same lump one vessel for honourable use, and another for common use?' (Rom. 9:18-21, NASB).

4. 'Election is conditional. God elected me because he knew all along that I would choose him.'

Some will admit that the Bible teaches election. But they believe that God's election of an individual is based on his pre-awareness of what that person would do.

Was there anything in us that merited God's electing love?

Once more, Paul calls this the 'election of grace'. If grace means 'unmerited favour', then the Bible clearly teaches that election is not based on anything either actually in, or fore-seen in, the creature who is chosen.

The natural tendency of the human heart is to expect to get what we deserve. In one of the scenes of *The Sound of Music,* the captain proposes to Maria (Julie Andrews). Maria is only a governess and the captain is a wealthy nobleman. Suddenly, Maria begins to sing. One of the lines in her musical response to the captain's proposal implies that she has 'done something good', in other words, she has somehow earnt her good fortune.

We would not expect God to love people like us. But, we reason, God couldn't love us unless we had done something, at some time in our life, that merited that love. The exciting message of this truth is that God does indeed love people who have nothing to offer him.

The apostle Paul zealously defends the unconditional nature of election by reminding us that God chose Jacob, 'the children not yet being born, nor having done any good or evil, that the purpose of God according to election might stand, not of works, but of him who calls' (Rom. 9:11). Election always depends on 'him who calls'. In other words, 'It is not of him who wills, nor of him who runs, but of God who shows mercy' (Rom. 9:16).

The same emphasis appears in Romans 11:6: 'And if [elec-tion is] by grace, then it is no longer of works [including fore-seen works]; otherwise grace is no longer grace.' 2 Timothy 1:9 is at pains to make clear that God's purpose, not our response, governs the universe. Ephesians 1:4-13 clearly teaches an election based solely on 'the purpose of him who works all things according to the counsel of his will' (1:11). God is not passive; he acts, not reacts.

Suppose you order a steak in a restaurant. How do you know you are going to be served a steak and not a hot dog? You know in advance what you are getting because it is what you ordered. Certainly God knows beforehand what will take place in his universe. But it is because he had already ordered it. Does a writer foresee the paper being covered with ink? Yes, but only because he or she has planned to put ink on the paper in the first place. Since none of us 'can come to [Christ] unless the Father ... draws him' (John 6:44), how could God foresee people coming to him apart from his call? Certainly,

God foresees people choosing him, but it is because God has first purposed and planned that they would choose him.

Romans 8:29 reads, 'For whom he foreknew, he also predestined.' This text is often used to support the idea that God foreknew who would believe and then predestined them. But look closely. Does the text actually say that God foreknew who would believe? Not at all. The verse simply says that those whom God knew before time, he predestined.

In Amos 3:2, God, speaking of Israel, says, 'You only have I known of all the families of the earth.' Does that mean God was not aware of Egypt's existence or that of other nations? The New American Standard Version translates 'known' here as 'chosen', recognizing a stronger meaning to the word than mere awareness. And like Israel, God has chosen us to follow him.

My move

Once I was assured that the Lord had chosen me, it became clear that I had to make a move. God had set his eternal gaze on me, awakened my heart to his grace, and I now realized that I could not passively sit back and watch 'the Spirit lead'. It was not so much a deliberate choice on my part — though it was certainly that — as it was a natural response from a heart that had been healed by God.

I decided to follow God for the rest of my life. And the changes God is bringing about in my life are in part what the next chapter considers.

5.
Election results

'All right, so maybe all this is in the Bible,' you may say, 'but I still don't understand how it relates to my life. It's all very well as a topic for debate to stretch our minds in an after-church fellowship, but does it really matter?'

Professor James Daane correctly perceives that 'Sermons on election are so rare that even a regular church-goer may never hear one... No other doctrine has been so central in theology and so ignored in the pulpit.'[1]

Once we leave the war room of theological debate and enter into a vital, honest and receptive dialogue with the Word of God, we will find ourselves falling in love all over again with the one who predestined us 'according to the counsel of his will' (Eph. 1:11). This application stage is just as important as the information stage. I do not believe that God is interested in whether we have accepted this doctrine if we have not made it a part of our lives. This truth must not only tell us that Christ is the Lord of our salvation; it must lead us to the point of experiencing his lordship and power in every segment of our lives.

Here are some of the practical results of believing that God is sovereign over salvation.

1. Humility

No other truth has had such a humbling effect on my own life as to realize that God makes the decisions about me. Read the following passage and I think you will see what I mean: 'God has chosen the foolish things of the world to shame the wise, and God has chosen the weak things of the world to shame the things which are strong, and the base things of the world and the despised, God has chosen, the things that are not, that he might nullify the things that are, that no man should boast before God. But by his doing you are in Christ Jesus ... that, just as it is written, "Let him who boasts, boast in the Lord"' (1 Cor. 1:27-31, NASB).

Knowing that we who believe are the elect of God teaches us that we are loved, though not lovely; chosen, though not choice; accepted, though not acceptable in ourselves. Because God's choice is not based on anything that he foresaw in us, there is no room for pride in being one of the elect.

Recently I discussed this subject with a close friend. He maintained that his salvation was not due to any 'good work' like baptism or church membership, but he was quick to insist that 'I'm saved because I said, "yes" to Christ.'

We can say, 'I'm saved because I ...' and it does not matter what comes after the 'because I'. If we can attribute our salvation to anything in our wills or actions (Rom. 9:16), ultimately, we have not been saved by grace; God is not the ultimate Author of our salvation.

Where I live you often see a bumper sticker that pleads with unbelievers to 'Give Jesus a Chance.' That is just what the proud heart wants to hear. But this theology of God's lordship in election shatters the image of a frustrated Saviour who wants us to let him in on the action. Another bumper sticker I have noticed goes so far as to say, 'Without you, God's plan is incomplete.' How's that for calling attention to number one? This man-centred, man-glorifying, God-defacing profanity must go! 'God is opposed to the proud, but gives grace to the humble' (James 4:6, NASB).

2. Appreciating God's grace

Jesus said, 'You did not choose me, but I chose you' (John 15:16). That gives me a great appreciation for God's grace, because it was God who first set his eyes on me. He wanted me. That is exciting!

One of the church's greatest problems today is that it has come to the place where it often takes God's grace for granted. Dietrich Bonhoeffer calls it 'cheap grace' and says,

'Cheap grace is the grace we bestow on ourselves.'[2] Isn't that an interesting comment? Well, if in fact, grace is something that we cannot bestow on ourselves — if, in other words, only God can grant grace — his is the most expensive type of grace on the market!

Election establishes a clear and certain proclamation of God's grace. After all, it ties salvation to God, not to human beings. Martin Luther said that Christians are absolutely required to know and preach this doctrine because 'of the knowledge of the grace of God'.

As this doctrine deflates our spiritual ego and checks our preoccupation with human achievement, we will find ourselves filled with a fresh sensitivity to our frailty and dependence upon God. And dependence upon him is the name of the game!

3. Commitment to holiness

The early church father Clement of Alexandria, (who lived in the second century), said, 'It is not becoming that one whom God has predestined before the foundation of the world to be put into the high adoption of children should fall into pleasures or fears, and be unemployed in repressing the passions.'

When we realize that we have been predestined to a holy calling, we sense a greater motivation to fulfil that calling. When we realize our destiny as being set apart from eternity to be a member of 'a chosen race, a royal priesthood, a holy nation, a people for God's own possession' (1 Peter 2:9, NASB), we begin to live life in the light of that purpose.

Why should we perform good works? Because God 'prepared beforehand that we should walk in them' (Eph. 2:10). Why should we persevere towards the goal of being conformed to Christ? Because we have been 'predestined to be conformed to the image of [God's] Son' (Rom. 8:29).

2 Thessalonians 2:13 reminds us that 'We are bound to give thanks to God always for you, brethren beloved by the Lord, because God from the beginning chose you for salvation through sanctification by the Spirit and belief in the truth.'

When I signed the original contract for the publication of this book, the agreement was that I would deliver an acceptable, completed copy to the publisher, even though the manuscript was still only a draft. God the Father contracted through his Son with the Holy Spirit that the Holy Spirit would present the Father with a perfect 'product'. And just as the process of presenting the publishers with a final copy takes various stages of editing and rewriting, so too our life is a process through which the Holy Spirit fulfils his contract by preparing us for the Father. Remember, God 'chose you for salvation *through* sanctification by the Spirit' (2 Thess. 2:13, italics mine). 'Just as he chose us in him ... that we should be holy' (Eph. 1:4).

In Colossians 3:12, election is mentioned as something that is vital for a holy life: 'And so, as those who have been chosen of God, holy and beloved, put on a heart of compassion, kindness, humility, gentleness and patience' (NASB). One more thing: because a knowledge of our election plunges us deeper into our relationship with God, our concern for, and perspective of, holiness will deepen as well. Instead of putting on a pious mask, I am now concerned about cultivating a holy lifestyle.

I want unbelievers to see that belonging to Christ changes my fundamental character — that now I am giving and loving, caring and forgiving. These are qualities that I am far from having mastered, but they are my goal as a child of God. To be holy means that I have been set apart as God's possession, and though I am distinct among other people, I am not isolated from them.

4. A healthy self-image

No sane person can look at this doctrine of election objectively and conclude, 'I'm worthless; a nobody — insignificant. No one cares what happens to me.'

I have a friend who means a great deal to me. I came home from college one summer, excited to see him again. I thought we could go around together just like old times. But he had decided that he wanted to be his own man. He was intentionally breaking away from our friendship. I would telephone and he would never call me back. So, with a fair dose of pride mingled with anger, I said, 'Fine. If that's what you want, it won't keep me awake at night!' But it did. We were close friends and I could not cope with the alienation. So I swallowed my pride, rang him again and asked him to meet me to talk about it. When he saw how much I cared about our friendship, his whole attitude changed. Our talk that afternoon ended with, 'What are we going to do tonight?'

God does not have any pride to swallow. He is the one for whom and by whom all things exist. Yet he stooped down to us in order to win back our friendship. We wanted to be out on our own. But God had different plans. If his choosing you does not let you know you are someone special, then nothing I could say would impress you with his love and care for you.

Also, because God's election has no strings attached ('it is not of him who wills, nor of him who runs, but of God who shows mercy,' Rom. 9:16), you can attach your sense of personal value and significance to the plan and purpose of a God who never changes, who is always stable, trustworthy and in charge. As Augustine said, 'God does not look for men fit to be elected; he makes them so.'

More and more believers and unbelievers in our modern technocracy are plagued with a low self-image. I can understand why unbelievers would have trouble accepting themselves; they have not as yet found acceptance from the one in whose image they were made — they have no identity in Christ. But how can believers, who trust in Christ for their salvation, be so preoccupied with self as to remain insecure? I am thoroughly convinced that it is because we have forgotten that God has 'predestined us to adoption as sons ... by which he has made us accepted in the Beloved' (Eph. 1:5-6). In his election God made us accepted. We don't have to win God's acceptance.

Fellow Christians, we can go through life confident — not self-confident — 'that he who has begun a good work in you will complete it' (Phil. 1:6). If we are 'predestined to be conformed to the image of [God's] Son' (Rom. 8:29), what more motivation do we need to go ahead and accept ourselves as God accepts us? 'Who shall bring a charge against God's elect?' (Rom. 8:32).

5. Blessed assurance

Nothing builds up our spiritual muscles quite like the assurance we have in being singled out as heirs of salvation —

knowing that God is ultimately the one who is governing our destiny. While the biblical message of election is threatening to those who refuse Christ, it is a harbinger of certainty and security for those who receive him.

Martin Luther underscored this truth so effectively: 'And if God be robbed of his power to elect, what will there be remaining but that idol, Fortune, under the name of which all things take place at random? Nay, we shall eventually come to this: that God has not determined by certain and glorious election who should be saved, but has left them to choose for themselves whether they shall be saved, while he, in the meantime, should be gone to an Ethiopian feast!'

'If therefore we are taught, and if we believe, that we do not need to know these things, Christian faith is utterly destroyed and the promises of God and the whole gospel entirely fall to the ground; for the greatest and only consolation and assurance for Christians in their adversity is that ... God does all things immutably and that his will cannot be resisted, changed, or hindered.'[3]

In other words, when God sets out to start a person's salvation, you can be sure that he will finish it!

If you are anything like me, a lot of things are uncertain in our lives as far as the future is concerned. But even in a world of overwhelming insecurities, we can know that God has fixed his eternal gaze on us and controls our destiny. This means we can get on with living life, unencumbered by the frustration, despair and uncertainty of the world around us.

6. Outspoken evangelism

You may be thinking, 'Election and evangelism — in the same breath? I've been told they are mutually exclusive!' I was told that too. But I can honestly say that telling the world about the gospel of Christ is the passion of my life. And the difference for me has been in seeing the doctrine of election more clearly. Election affects evangelism in three major areas: our message, our methods and our motivation.

Firstly, how does election affect the *message*? Election does not allow us, in good conscience, to tell unbelievers, 'You can make it, with God's help.' Election makes us tell the truth. It does indeed drive sinners to despair by suggesting that they cannot be saved by their own power. But, after all, if the gospel we preach does not do that, then it is not the Christian gospel.

When we announce to people, '*I* found it!' we give the impression that God was lost, not us. I see the lapel pin, 'Try God,' in many places, as if God was just another experience or another way out. To people who have tried just about everything else from EST to Eastern Meditation, now we bring out the true God for a test drive.

We need to turn from our bargain-basement, man-centred slogans and tell people the truth. *We* don't find God on our own; *we* don't give God a chance. The apostles never preached in such terms. No matter what sinful men and women choose they have to be assured that their destiny is always in God's hands. They love God because he has first loved them!

In my own witnessing, I sometimes encounter people who say, 'Maybe some day.' That is because I have failed to inform that person that 'some day' belongs to God. We have no control over tomorrow. We do not know if there will be an earthquake or a nuclear war. Something less dramatic might take our life: perhaps a road accident or cancer. The point is that we do not control our own destiny. Our only hope, then, is to come humbly before the throne of Christ, the one who *does* hold our future, acknowledging that 'It is not of him who wills, nor of him who runs, but of God who shows mercy' (Rom. 9:16).

The apostle Paul made sure that people of his day heard the fulness of their hope: 'But by *his* doing you are in Christ Jesus' (1 Cor. 1:30, NASB, italics mine). And Jesus said, 'You did not choose me, but I chose you, and 'Without me you can do nothing' (John 15:16, 5).

Today, we are trying to reconcile God to men and women, rather than reconcile men and women to God. Our converts are weak because they are depending on their own will and their own ability to trust in order to get them where they know they need to be. Their faith is weak because they are constantly looking at themselves and drawing upon their own resources — their willpower, faith and piety. With election as the backdrop, the Lord Jesus Christ becomes the centre of attention. After all, he is the one who holds the keys of eternal life. Thus, Jesus Christ thundered from heaven, 'I am alive for evermore... I have the keys of Hades and of Death' (Rev. 1:18). The one who has the keys is the one who opens the door of salvation to us. With our destiny in his control, trusting in Christ is not so difficult after all.

Secondly, how does election affect our *methods*? Sometimes, as I have gone witnessing with a group of people, I have wondered whether I was sharing Christ or selling a line of products. It is interesting to see how some of the cults have picked up Christian formulas and patterns of communicating. These cult members are so predictable that we can see them coming a mile off. Like us, they tend to offer simplistic formulas, but unlike us they cannot know a God who calls people to himself.

Because of election, we realize that as Christians we do not have to resort to such desperate tactics. We know that in the final analysis, it is God's electing grace, not our techniques, that determines the outcome of our presentation. With this knowledge we can be more comfortable and free in our witnessing to friends and family. While we have the responsibility to bring them the gospel, in word and deed, they will not go to hell because we failed to cover all the basic points. Instead, we participate in God's plan for bringing people into his kingdom, knowing that it is God's Spirit, not our personality or persuasion, who ultimately brings a person to Christ.

2,000 years ago, Jesus told the woman at the well that his Father is *seeking* people to worship him. That is still just as true today!

Finally, how does election affect our *motivation*? What is the impact of election on evangelism? Paul, the greatest missionary the church ever had, said, 'I endure all things for the sake of the elect, that they also may obtain the salvation which is in Christ Jesus with eternal glory' (2 Tim. 2:10). He pushed on from city to city motivated by God's assurance: 'I have many people in this city' (Acts 18:10).

William Carey, often called the founder of the modern missionary movement, considered election, and its related concepts, to be what undergirded his whole enterprise. David Livingstone and many others concurred with him in this.

Have you ever felt despondent over all there is to do for Christ? A missionary was flying over Bombay, India, and saw the massive crowds dotting the scene beneath him. At first he wanted to turn back. 'Look at all those people!' he gasped. 'I won't even make a dent.' Then he remembered that God had not called him to save India. God had called him to preach the gospel of Jesus Christ in India; God would do the saving work. That thought, the missionary said, brought him out of the frustration and despair so that he could work for God without encumbrance.

Charles Spurgeon was, and is, considered to be the greatest evangelist of his time. He packed giant halls with people who needed to hear his message and was so inspired by his conviction of God's sovereignty that he concluded, 'This is the gospel!' Thousands responded. George Whitefield, John Newton, Hudson Taylor and countless missionaries and evangelists could echo the same excitement.

When I tell a group of people about Christ, I know that what I am doing is important; that it really counts in history, as well as in eternity. It counts because while I am preaching, God is at work in people's hearts. I do not know which people God is speaking to inwardly, but I realize that I am an essential part of God's plan to bring his elect into his kingdom through the preaching of his Word.

Some people find it hard to understand why God needs people to evangelize if he has already made his decision. The answer is, God does not need us; he has nevertheless chosen to use us. God has not only decided whom he will save, but how he will save them. Evangelism, prayer, the reading and preaching of the Word — these are all 'modes of transportation' that God has ordained for bringing his people to himself.

A. W. Pink said, 'God is not working at random; the gospel has been sent forth on no uncertain mission.' Because salvation is a mission accomplished, evangelism works!

I have found that I am excited to tell others about the gospel because now I have something substantial to present. I used to be forced to give a plan of salvation without a plan for salvation but not any more.

7. A desire to worship

We evangelicals are in a dry period when it comes to worship. Our services are often attempts to entertain or simply to keep the faithful occupied. Many of us meet in lecture halls with music on Sunday mornings. Where have the majesty of worship and the participation of God's people gone? Preaching today is man-centred. It glorifies us more than God. Our preaching is geared more towards making people happy than towards calling them to worship God. Hence we talk more about relationships, retreats and other social aspects of church life than we do about worship.

I do not believe there is anything wrong with Christian fellowship. In fact, we need deeper, more profound communion among people in our congregations. And I love retreats. They are great opportunities to get away and to gain a new perspective. But these are not worship.

Worship is an attitude, a frame of mind, and a response on the part of the creature triggered by an attribute or action of the Creator. The basic premise of worship is that God is King and Lord of everything — including our salvation and destiny — and we are to praise God for that.

Since my journey began, back in my early teens, I have read and reread Scriptures relating to God's sovereign power to save and sustain us. I can honestly say that my worship life deepens with every reading. At times my sense of awe, respect and admiration for God is uncontainable. That is what joy is all about. Joyful living is a life of worship; and worship involves all of life.

Cold orthodoxy is the result of absorbing doctrine without gratitude. Emotionalism is the result of gratitude without doctrine. We need both. The former tendency lends to an obsession with intellectual data without expression through love, charity, good works and free worship. The latter is like saying, 'Thank you' 142 times, without exactly knowing why. Let us recognize our dependence upon God and not hesitate to worship God in response.

8. Commitment to the supernatural

Election reminds us that we do not become Christians by any natural process. Election demonstrates that salvation is supernatural, divinely executed. It shows us that God interrupts the natural and speaks, acts and moves in history.

Election also shows us that God is free, and not governed by the choices and conditions of his creatures or frustrated by 'accidents'.

Many of us have been taught to spurn the supernatural or even deny miracles when they happen because our theology does not allow for the possibility of God's intervention in nature. But God assures us, 'I will have mercy on whomever I will have mercy, and I will have compassion on whomever I will have compassion' (Rom. 9:15). That simply means that if God wants to do something special for someone, he will. God's sovereignty teaches us that 'With God, all things are possible' (Matt. 19:26).

This means we can pray with power!

Election and the Bible

This doctrine affects both believers and unbelievers in many other positive ways. But the most significant reason that election should be recognized, understood and proclaimed is that it is a major theme of Scripture. Martin Luther said that this doctrine was as clearly revealed in Scripture 'as the very notion of a Supreme Being'.

John R. W. Stott writes, 'The doctrine of election is the product of Divine revelation, not human speculation. It was not invented by Calvin of Geneva or Augustine of Hippo. It is above all else a Biblical doctrine and no Biblical Christian can ignore it.'[4]

Wherever election appears in Scripture, it is taken for granted as a truth. Only in a few places is election argued or defended. Normally, it simply 'appears' as a premise. It undergirds the whole redemptive story and gives it design, form and purpose.

Here are a few passages to illustrate the point:

> The counsel of the Lord stands for ever....
> Blessed [are] ...
> the people whom he has chosen as his own
>   inheritance
>
>   (Ps. 33:11-12).

Blessed is the man whom you ...
cause to approach you,
That he may dwell in your courts!

(Ps. 65:4).

'Oh, visit me with your salvation,
That I may see the benefit of your chosen
    ones'

(Ps. 106:4-5).

'Every plant which my heavenly Father has
    not planted will be uprooted'

(Matt. 15:13).

'Shall not God avenge his own elect?'

(Luke 18:7).

'As many as had been appointed to eternal life
    believed'

(Acts 13:48).

Understanding this doctrine unlocks many of the hidden meanings of Scripture, and 'mysteries' turn into revelations.

How do I know if I am one of the elect?

Not only are we told to make our calling and election sure (2 Peter 1:10), we are also told how to do it. In 1 Thessalonians 1:4 Paul spoke of 'knowing, beloved brethen, your election by God'. Then he tells us why he knew they were 'elect': 'For our gospel did not come to you in word only, but also in power, and in the Holy Spirit and in much assurance ... And you became followers of us and of the Lord' (1 Thess. 1:5-6). Christ said, 'My sheep hear my voice, and I know them, and they follow me' (John 10:27). Romans 8:30 reads, 'Moreover whom he predestined, these he also called.'

Have you been called? Have you believed? Did the gospel come to you in more than word only? Did it come to you with 'much assurance'? Are you a follower of Christ, one who has heard his voice and acted on it as a command for daily living?

Then you have made your calling and election sure. If not, then respond to the invitation of Christ in his Word: 'Come to me, all you who labour and are heavy laden, and I will give you rest' (Matt. 11:28).

6.
Close encounters

Our salvation is rooted in our being chosen by God before the world even began. But things did not end there — divine election was only the start.

God was faced with the matter of somehow transmitting all that he had chosen to do into the realm of time and space. God needed to come to us. Someone once said that Christianity is not a religion because religion is men and women trying to reach God; Christianity is God successfully reaching men and women. The story of the Tower of Babel (see Genesis 11) demonstrates the human longing to reach God; but in reaching out for him, they only grasped confusion and frustration.

God's decision to choose us was not enough. It was more complicated than that. We still could not make any moves towards God. So God made the ultimate move towards us by sending his Son. The incarnation (God the Son becoming human) is the most eloquent testimony to how seriously God took his election of us.

The council of the triune Godhead — Father, Son and Holy Spirit — determined that the second person of the Trinity, called in Scripture the Word of God, would be the mediator between God and man. God, the eternal Son, would become human.

Suppose, for the sake of illustration, that one week after you pick up your brand-new car from the showroom someone steals it. You want your car back. You determine not to rest until the car is returned. You notify the police and insurance company and take all possible steps to trace it.

A week passes. Nothing happens. Then a phone call comes telling you that the car has been located over two hundred miles away. The car has been damaged, but it can be repaired and driven home. You breathe a sigh of relief. You decided to pull out all the stops to get the car back, executed your plan to find it, and the plan worked. But your mission still is not complete. Now, either you or someone else has to travel the two hundred miles to get the car, get it repaired and bring it home.

Any thorough discussion of the role of divine election in our salvation is similarly incomplete if it ends up only in the philosophical realm of God's choosing or finding his people in eternity. The fact is, God also had to send someone to get us. This is always the way it is. God comes to us and brings us back. We aren't even looking for God, but God is obsessed with finding us.

Is God hiding?

Theologians often used to refer to the '*Deus Absconditus*' — the veiled God. When Moses beheld the glory of God, he had to cover his face when he returned to the people down below. Always, it seems to us, God is 'up there', removed from the human scene. One thing that the incarnation teaches us is that ours is a personal God — a divine Being, an almighty, transcendent God, to be sure; but personal none the less. Just as the theology of 'the hidden God' was dominating the minds of men and women, God broke through the silence, humbled himself in the person of the divine Son and contradicted all our objections against God's apparent ignorance of, or sympathy for, human existence.

John Boys, a Puritan divine, said, 'The best way to reconcile two disagreeing families is to make some marriage between them: even so, the Word became flesh and dwelt among us in the world that he might hereby make our peace, reconciling man to God. By this happy match the Son of God is become the Son of Man, even flesh of our flesh, and bone of or bones.'[1]

The living Word

The book of Hebrews offers a profound insight into the
mission of this divine Word, the Son of God: 'God, after he
spoke long ago to the fathers in the prophets in many portions
and in many ways, in these last days has spoken to us in his
Son, whom he appointed heir of all things, through whom
also he made the world' (Heb. 1:1-2, NASB). That scripture
sends shivers down my spine — to think that the same Word
who created us came to us at a point in history as one of us!

Thus, we compare the opening of Genesis, where God
created the world through his Word, to the opening of the
Gospel of John: 'In the beginning was the Word, and the
Word was with God, and the Word was God. He was in the
beginning with God. All things came into being through him;
and apart from him nothing came into being that has come
into being. In him was life; and the life was the light of men.
And the light shines in the darkness; and the darkness did not
comprehend it' (John 1:1-5, NASB).

Here the 'Word' is still Jesus Christ, but the 'light' has come
to us in human flesh. Without diminishing his deity, Christ
has assumed our humanity. Thus, John writes that 'The Word
became flesh and dwelt among us', and that 'The darkness did
not comprehend it' (John 1:14,5). The creatures did not recognize their Creator. He came to our home and we did not
welcome him.

So the Son has come to carry out the will of the Father;
divine election has taken on flesh and blood. The Father has
selected the inhabitants of his royal priesthood, the Son has
come in obedience as the Servant to redeem them and the
Holy Spirit works in our hearts to cause us to respond in faith.

To understand the practical implications of Christ's coming
to earth for us, let me address this matter from three vantage-
points: God with us, God in us and God through us.

God with us

When we say that Christ is the 'Word' of God, we are saying
that Christ is the eternal wisdom *(logos)* of the Father. Christ
became the 'translator' between God and a fallen world that

could not speak his language. Trying to understand God apart from his 'Word' is like trying to understand a foreign nation without its ambassador. We are finite and limited in our reason and will, and our nature is blinded by self-centredness and sin. Therefore, the mediator had to be God, so he could tell us the truth about the Father. Yet he also had to be one of us so that truth could be communicated to fallen beings. Hence Christ is the bridge from the infinite to the finite. Jesus was, and is God saying, 'Here I am! This is what I'm like.' John called him 'God's only begotten Son' (John 3:16). Isaiah proclaimed him, 'Mighty God' (Isa. 9:6). Matthew called him 'Immanuel, … God with us' in the flesh.

During one of my childhood crises, I ran into my room and slammed the door behind me. I just wanted to be alone and to shut the world out. (We seem to think problems will go away if we just have a little time to ourselves.) Before long, my dad knocked on the door and said, 'Son, can I come in?'

'Dad,' I answered, 'believe me, there's nothing you can do to help me right now.'

You see, there was this girl at school whom I happened to like. But she did not even know I existed — unless of course, she saw me when I tripped over my own shadow watching her every move. How could Dad, above all people, understand what I was going through? Finally, however, at his insistence I opened the door and opened up to him, telling him all about my frustrations. I was really shocked. He understood my problem! Why? Because he had once been in exactly the same situation. He told me about a girl named Mary when he was at school.

Nothing in the world is worse than someone who tells you, 'I know just how you feel,' when you know that he or she doesn't have the faintest idea about what is going on inside you. But when people can really identify with your experience, they earn the right to advise you.

The doctrine historically called the incarnation is all about God the Son's meeting us by becoming one of us. And by this act and its subsequent accomplishments, he did not leave us. Jesus Christ came to show us what God is like and left a sympathizer for the human condition. As Judge, he cannot condone our weaknesses; but as one of us, he can understand them.

God the Son, Jesus Christ, earned his right to a place in our lives because he went through everything we go through. Nobody understands human life like Jesus Christ! 'For we do not have a High Priest who cannot sympathize with our weaknesses, but was in all points tempted as we are, yet without sin' (Heb. 4:15). Though he never sinned, he faced the devil, all the temptations that we do and even death on our behalf.

The incarnation of the Son of God gives us a fuller understanding of the reign of God over us. And in it we see that God belongs in our everyday world: eating, drinking, resting, working, socializing with us, telling us about the Father and his plan of redemption and giving us a vision for his kingdom.

Many of us are clear on our doctrine of Christ's deity: Jesus was and is fully God. But is Jesus now isolated 'up there', removed from the mundane, common, daily affairs of average people? No, he is also — along with the Father and the Holy Spirit — really present with us.

Doesn't God spend most of his time thinking about heads of state or presidents of major corporations? No, Immanuel means 'God with us', not 'God with them'. But isn't God really close to the professional religious people? Don't they have 'a hot line' to God? Not at all. Where did Jesus spend his time on earth? With publicans and sinners. Those were his friends.

Granted, many of us who are believers have appeared 'out of touch' with the world. But Jesus Christ is anything but detached. While it may be said with some truthfulness that many Christians have their feet firmly planted in the air, Christ was at the centre of human life, revealing where God's heart is drawn. He attended dinners, weddings, funerals, feasts, or simply 'nights out' with people. That has a tendency to offend me, especially when I'm feeling particularly 'pious'. Jesus saw this 'holier than thou' attitude as most unholy.

We are offended to find the Holy One meeting people at a party of former tax-collectors, frauds, eating and drinking with them, or conversing with a prostitute, treating her as if she were a princess, while never once even remotely condoning her ways! The religious leaders soon labelled Jesus as one who ate 'with tax collectors and sinners' (Matt. 9:11). For these leaders religion was a shelter from the 'less desirable'

out there in the world. Religion did not go where the alienated people, the broken, uncomforted hearts needed it most.
Jesus changed that fatal tradition.

When Jesus lived on earth Augustus Cæsar was in power.
He was a man who claimed to be a god; Jesus was the true
God who had in fact become a man. In the Garden of Eden,
Adam and Eve gave in to sin because they wanted to be like
God. While we are constantly reaching out for independence,
God the Son teaches us to depend on the Father, as he did.
Just as we think we are getting ahead, climbing up the ladder,
Jesus comes and tells us that true happiness is found by
heading in the other direction!

The incarnation also contradicted the expectations of Israel.
Could the King of kings really be a baby lying in a feeding
basin for livestock? How could the Creator and Ruler of the
universe be the man who had nowhere to lay his head at
night? 'Is this not the carpenter's son? Is not his mother called
Mary? And his brothers, James, Joses, Simon, and Judas?'
(Matt. 13:55). In essence, people were asking, 'He is just a
normal, average person; how could somebody like that be
God in the flesh?' Because the Father wanted it that way. In
the beauty of the nativity we witness God who is *with* us. The
one who chose us is not only above us: God is with us.

God in us

It would have been exciting enough if God had only been with
us: exciting, yes, but not enough to change our present condition. Not only does the incarnation teach us that God came
to us and lived *with* us; it also teaches us that through our
union with Christ, God can live *within* us! Jesus Christ can
take up residence in the humble manger of our hearts.

Because of the mystery of the incarnation, the Holy Spirit
can live within us. 'Do you not know that you are the temple
of God and that the Spirit of God dwells in you?' (1 Cor.
3:16).

When Jesus was born almost 2,000 years ago, he initiated a
new human nature. Whereas we were under the headship of
Adam, now we could be brought under the headship of

Christ. When he is born within us, we gain a new nature — we are joined to the glorified humanity of the resurrected Christ.

Just as God with us changed the shape of the world for ever, God in us changes the shape of our lives for ever. No longer are we despairing. We may have shortcomings and frustration, but we never despair.

Nothing is more fulfilling for a Christian than to have someone say, 'I can sense something different about you.' What that person sees is God in us: 'To them God willed to make known what are the riches of the glory of this mystery among the Gentiles: which is Christ in you, the hope of glory' (Col. 1:27).

God through us

Still, it would not be enough if God were merely with us and in us. The Bible teaches that God has even more ambitious plans, that God's programme includes not just us, but also has implications for the people around us. We spend too much of our time as Christians on things of self-interest. Of course, that is where our culture is right now. Self-improvement — whether in the areas of beauty maintenance, psychoanalysis, self-hypnosis, health and fitness, or similar topics — is a hunger of our society that feels it has now 'come of age'. Even the general headings of much Christian literature today show that many believers are preoccupied with their own condition.

We talk endlessly about our personal relationship with Jesus Christ. But what about everybody else out there? Are we so busy 'preening our feathers' that we don't take time to consider the implications of Christ through us, changing the world?

We need our Christian community life, but cannot help wondering whether we have become more of a closed society than a community. We are not vulnerable to the world, nor even all that accessible, as the Author of our faith was. We are afraid to be offended by evil, paranoid that the world is, inch by inch, going to get too close to us; so we pick up stones to cast at sinners rather than reaching out to them in compassion. The incarnation does not come to a full stop with you and me! The same baby in the manger, the same one who lives on high, the same Christ who lives within you, now wants to live his life *through* you. Because of our community, the world should be forced to confess, 'Jesus is alive. These people are forming his body.'

God has a tremendous plan for this world and he has made believers indispensable to the working out of the plan. 'It is God who works in you both to will and to do for his good pleasure' (Phil. 2:13). Now that God has come to us and lives within us, we have a responsibility to participate in his mission.

Let us also remember that Jesus' incarnation was miraculous. Mary, a blessed and highly esteemed instrument, could claim no contribution to her mysterious conception, other than to say, 'Let it be to me according to your word' (Luke 1:38). Just as Mary asked, 'How can this be, since I do not know a man?' (Luke 1:34), so we must ask in wonder, 'How can it be that Jesus could be conceived within my soul?'

The answer for us is the same as it was for Mary: 'The Holy Spirit will come upon you, and the power of the Highest will overshadow you' (Luke 1:35). God living with us, in us and through us because of the incarnation, is all a miracle.

7.
He got what he paid for

'Behold! The Lamb of God who takes away the sin of the world!' (John 1:29). That proclamation celebrates the theme before us: the most obvious and profound demonstration of God's love and grace manifested in the sacrifice of Jesus Christ for our offences. Frederick W. Norwood said, 'The cross is central. It struck into the middle of the world, into the middle of time, into the middle of destiny. The cross is struck into the heart of God.'

God's plan is to save this world by taking people from every nation and forming a new body of humanity. Christ proved that God's heart was drawn to all people — not just the religious or the people in high places, but to men, women and children of every interest, position, colour, race and nationality. God is not a racist. 'Red and yellow, black and white; they are precious in his sight' is not just a cute little line from a children's hymn. The words express a profound truth illustrated in the cross. All people will be saved.

'Ah, wait a moment!' someone will say. That sounds as if I am supporting universalism — i.e. saying that everybody will eventually be saved. Not at all! But while we who take the Scriptures seriously do not believe that each and every person in the world will be saved, we must be universalists in the sense that we are forced to view God's programme as being broader than encompassing only individuals. In a sense, God sees the world as a community of mankind, a unit. Christ came not only 'to save sinners' (1 Tim. 1:15). He came also to be the 'Saviour of the world' (John 4:42).

In John 3:17, we notice the universal side of Christ's mission: 'For God did not send his Son into the world to condemn the world, but that the world through him might be saved.' The next verse says, 'He who believes in him is not condemned; but he who does not believe is condemned already, because he has not believed in the name of the only begotten Son of God.' Verse 17 focuses on the world as a unit, mankind as a race, while verse 18 views the world on the individual level. So God is concerned about saving individuals, and God is also concerned about saving the world he created. Let me explain what I mean.

Eventually sin will be removed from creation, and we shall start all over again. Christ, by his death, secured the purging not only of persons but the whole creation. Hence, Christ 'takes away the sin of the world'. And notice that he does not make possible the removal of the world's sin: he actually accomplishes it! We can be confident that Christ secured the redemption of individuals (new creatures) as well as of creation (a new heaven and a new earth). The world, fallen in Adam, is restored in Christ.

One of the most shocking and divisive doctrines of early Christianity was the universality of God's plan, the fact that it was not limited to one ethnic group (Israel). The Jews had always considered the Messiah's work in terms of restoring the nation of Israel, not in terms of his restoring the souls of people in all nations. This misunderstanding is nowhere better outlined than in John 11:50-52: 'One man should die for the people, and not that the whole nation should perish... He prophesied that Jesus would die for the nation, and not for that nation only, but also that he would gather together in one the children of God who were scattered abroad.'

Later, in 1 John 2:2, the same disciple wrote of Christ, 'He ... is the propitiation for our sins, and not for ours only but also for the whole world.'

The atoning work of our God knows no boundaries set by tradition, nationality, period in time, economic or political restrictions. God's atoning work is for everyone!

Saviour of the body

I often talk about missions and evangelism in terms of 'winning the world to Christ', as do many other Christians. Does that mean that I believe everyone in the world will be won to Christ? No. It simply means that I recognize the universal implications of the gospel. The cross is to be taken to everyone everywhere because everyone is responsible for accepting its message or rejecting it.

Salvation, then, is universal in that it crosses all barriers and includes every kind of person, but not in the sense that it includes each and every individual.

Perhaps this sounds like a contradiction, but bear with me. I can talk about world peace without every individual being at peace with his or her neighbour; or I can speak of world hunger while much of the world eats balanced meals. I love God's universe, but I hate evil, Satan and his allies. The 'world' does not always mean every individual inclusively, but rather the world as a general entity.

Luke records that 'all the world' was taxed by Cæsar Augustus (2:1), but obviously not every single individual in the world at that time was taxed by Augustus. The Pharisees said of Christ, 'Look, the world has gone after him!'(John 12:19), but it is clear from many other statements that not every single person in the world had gone after him.

In the latter part of Romans, Paul wrote that 'All Israel will be saved' (11:26). A little earlier he had written that only 'a remnant according to the election of grace' (11:5) would be saved out of Israel. He then proceeds to show us that 'all Israel is saved' by means of an elect remnant. If 'all Israel will be saved ... [via] a remnant according to the election of grace,' then why can we not say that 'All the world will be saved via a remnant chosen by grace'? This, I believe, is the intent of John 3:16: God loved the world so much that he sent his Son to save all believers (not those who will die in unbelief). His mission was to save the world, not condemn it. And because of the elect international remnant, the world is, in fact, saved! The human family is not lost, but continues its lineage through a new spiritual race: the kingdom of God.

When we view the cross in its universal implications, then, we see a planet that Christ has come to reclaim: 'For the earnest expectation of the creation eagerly waits for the revealing of the sons of God... The creation itself also will be delivered from the bondage of corruption into the glorious liberty of the children of God. For we know that the whole creation groans and labours with birth pangs together until now... Even we ... eagerly [await] the adoption, the redemption of our body' (Rom. 8:19, 21-23).

Yet when we view the cross in its individual implications, we recognize that Jesus saved 'his people from their sins' (Matt. 1:21). Both the world and people in that world are actually saved. Hence, Christ is the Saviour of the world and the Saviour of the body (the church).

I was writing this book during the summer when the Olympics were held in Los Angeles. We were repeatedly told that 'The world is on our doorstep.' Now, I like to have company, and I like to be with people about as much as the next man. But I would be really worried if I thought that by that statement it was meant that every man, woman, boy and girl on planet Earth would literally be 'on my doorstep'. But of course what people really meant was that people from every nation were at our doorstep.

While God's plan involves the salvation of the world, that remnant representing the world forms the bride of Christ. And there is no redemption apart from saying, 'I do.'

For whom did Christ die?

Dr Robert Lightner states that 'It is doubtful if a more important question could be asked' than this, though he disagrees with the conclusion I have reached. In defining the extent of the atonement (i.e. how many are included) we can discover the nature, character and results of the atonement.

Every orthodox Christian places limits on the work of Christ. If Jesus died for every individual, but not every individual is saved, then his death did not actually save anybody. Thus, the work of Christ is limited in its power. If, however, the atonement, though sufficient for each and every individual, was made on behalf of the chosen people, the church, that atonement is limited in its scope or purpose. If Christ died for people who will be in hell, his efforts cannot accurately be called a 'saving work'. Dr Lewis Sperry Chafer said, 'Christ's death does not save either actually or potentially;

rather it makes all men savable.'[1] If that is true, there is no real power in the blood. Rather, the power would seem to be in the will of the creature.

Along with many other believers, I label my position 'definite atonement'. 'Atonement is defined in the dictionary as 'satisfaction made'. Definite means 'a specific intention that is neither vague nor general'. That, I believe, is the atonement we find in Scripture: 'satisfaction made that has a specific intention that is neither vague nor general'.

Christ came with a mission from the Father. And that mission was in fact accomplished at Calvary. All of us as Christians are interested in what was (or was not) accomplished at the cross. For upon that premise our very salvation depends.

These points lie at the heart of the Christian message, for they rest at the foot of the cross. Far from being mere items for scholarly debate, the questions 'For whom did Christ die?' and 'For what did Christ die?' form the basis of the Christian hope. If we consider 'Jesus paid it all' to be more than a nice song; if our salvation was secured 'at the cross' and if we are expected to 'crown him [Jesus] with many crowns', rather than crowning our Saviour for paving the way for redemption while crowning ourselves for 'appropriating' it, then we shall have to wrestle with this matter.

Was Christ's sacrifice an attempt to save everybody? Or was it a success in saving 'his people from their sins'? (Matt. 1:21). The Scriptures declare, 'He has ... accomplished redemption for his people' (Luke 1:68, NASB). Nowhere is it said in even the vaguest terms, 'He has made all men savable.'

Christians have historically believed in God in terms of a Trinity: three in person, one in essence — Father, Son and Holy Spirit. The Father elects and designs the programme, the Son executes it by securing the destiny of the elect and the Holy Spirit gives life to their spirits, uniting them through faith to Jesus Christ. Let's look at the work of Christ, then, in terms of the purpose of the Father, Son and Holy Spirit.

8.
God's eternal purpose

Part of the problem we have in coming to this discussion is that we are inclined to view Christ's work as distinct and, in fact, detached from, the work of the Father and Spirit. The heavenly Father has designed and is governing the plan of redemption. Christ was sent by the Father to accomplish the Father's purpose. So what is that purpose?

When did God give his Son as our sacrifice? He was 'slain', said John, 'from the foundation of the world' (Rev. 13:8). The meaning of this statement can be understood only in the light of a corresponding passage, Ephesians 1:4: 'Just as he [the Father] chose us in him [the Son] before the foundation of the world, that we should be holy and without blame before him.' In the mind of the eternal Father, the Lamb without blemish had already been sacrificed when he had chosen the heirs of redemption and had placed them in Christ for eternity.

The Father's purpose

Before the world existed, the Scriptures tell us, God selected a large number of people out of the human race that he would create to be his sons and daughters. 'For whom he foreknew, he also predestined' (Rom. 8:29). God set his eternal gaze upon them. This work of Christ is based on the covenant between Father and Son, establishing the Son as the head and trustee of the Father's new people. Shedding blood was always an act of atonement on behalf of 'the people' (the covenant community) in the Old Testament. Never was the sacrificial system designed to remit the sins of those outside the covenant. In the New Testament, that same covenant continues. Christ has been made the ultimate sacrifice for the sins of 'the people', although now that group includes people in every part of the globe, not just the nation of Israel. Because of this particular relationship of the covenant to the will of the Father in salvation, Christ's atonement is called 'the blood of the everlasting covenant' (Heb. 13:20).

The Father's plan, therefore, is selective; not everyone is chosen. 'We are bound to give thanks to God always for you, brethren beloved by the Lord, because God from the beginning chose you for salvation' (2 Thess. 2:13). And Peter wrote that we were 'elect ... for obedience and sprinkling of the blood of Jesus Christ' (1 Peter 1:2). 'Just as he *chose* us in him,' it is 'in him [that] we have *redemption* through his blood' (Eph. 1:4, 7, italics mine). If the Father places some — indeed, many — in Christ to 'be holy and without blame before him' (Eph. 1:4), then we must agree that the rest are not chosen and placed in Christ to be holy and without blame before him. In fact, Scripture identifies these as 'vessels of wrath prepared for destruction' (Rom. 9:22). Would Christ have died to save 'vessels of wrath prepared for destruction'?

So we do indeed have a definite election, a particular election. God has decreed in his rich and peculiar grace to save a great number of people from all over the world, from every walk of life. But those who were not placed 'in Christ' by the Father were not redeemed 'by Christ' at the cross. 'Who shall bring a charge against God's elect?' Paul asked (Rom. 8:33). After all, he concluded, 'It is Christ who died' to remove all charges from God's chosen people (Rom. 8:34). This doctrine has no place for self-condemnation!

The Son's purpose

1 Peter 1:2 says that believers are 'elect ... for ... sprinkling of the blood of Jesus Christ'. When you go to the shop and select some fruit from the display, do you end up buying all the fruit, or only the fruit you choose to take home? Is it possible for the Father to have one purpose and the Son to have yet another? Could Christ outdo the Father's generosity by enlarging on the scope of redemption's plan?

If we are to understand the doctrine of the Trinity in orthodox terms, it is absolutely impossible for the scope, intent and purpose of the Son to differ in any way from the Father's. I often hear it said, 'It's no longer a sin issue, but a Son issue.' The intention of this phrase is to suggest that the sinner is condemned — not on the basis of the person's many sins (since Christ has atoned for them), but because he or she has rejected Christ. Hence, some say, Christ has assumed the debt for everyone and cleared everyone of all sins; but if an individual rejects this gracious provision, he or she will be condemned on the basis of that rejection.

We can see how this view fails to take into account the fact that rejecting Christ is itself a sin. I can see no distinction whatsoever between a 'sin issue and a Son issue'. Rejecting Christ is simply one of many millions of sins for which people will be condemned. 'He who does not believe is condemned already,' Jesus announced (John 3:18). And Paul lists a number of particular sins: 'fornication, uncleanness, passion, evil desire, and covetousness, which is idolatry,' and concludes that 'Because of these things the wrath of God is coming' (Col. 3:5, 6) — not simply because of unbelief.

If Christ's sacrifice covers each and every individual — even those who will never accept it — we are faced with two alternatives: either to say that everyone without exception will be saved (since there is no longer any basis for condemnation, all sins being cancelled) or that there is one sin (unbelief) for which Christ did not atone.

Here is an important point. Christ said, 'I have come down from heaven, not to do my own will, but the will of him who sent me. This is the will of the Father who sent me, that of all he has given me I should lose nothing, but should raise it up at the last day' (John 6:38-39). This passage either teaches universal salvation or definite atonement; but plainly whoever it is that the Father has given to Christ will receive eternal life. And if Christ has come 'not to do my own will, but the will of him who sent me', then the purpose of the Son must be just as limited in scope as the Father's.

Our Saviour tells us precisely that. On one occasion in particular, Jesus was conversing with some Pharisees. He knew they were not responsive to his teachings, and he told them twice: 'I lay down my life for the sheep,' and then boldly informed them, 'But you do not believe, because you are not of my sheep' (see John 10:15, 17, 26). And a few hours before the crucifixion, Jesus prayed to the Father: 'You have given [me] authority over all flesh, that [I] should give eternal life to as many as you have given [me] ... I do not pray *for the world* but for those whom you have given me' (John 17:2, 9). Though Christ was delegated 'authority over all mankind', he chose to focus his saving atonement on his covenant family: 'those whom you have given [me]'. Scripture says Christ died 'to purify for himself his own special people' (Titus 2:14). Hebrews makes clear that it was Christ's intention to '[bring] many sons to glory' (2:10). The Saviour said, 'Here am I and the children whom God has given me' (Heb. 2:13), and he 'led captivity captive' (Eph. 4:8).

The Holy Spirit's purpose

In Romans 8:30, it is said that those ' whom he predestined, these he also called' effectively by God's Spirit into fellowship and communion with the Trinity, although everyone is invited to come. Furthermore, Christ said *his* sheep hear his voice, and Christ 'called us with a holy calling ... according to his own purpose and grace which was given to us in Christ Jesus before time began' (2 Tim. 1:9). In Acts 13:48 we read that 'As many as had been appointed to eternal life believed.' The witness of Scripture appears clear and emphatic in its description of a specific design for salvation.

Did Christ buy back more people than the Holy Spirit intends to bring back?

But doesn't God love everybody?

In Romans 9, Jacob is used to illustrate the elect of God, and Esau is used to illustrate the non-elect. Jacob is loved and Esau is hated 'that the purpose of God according to election might stand, not of works but of him who calls' (9:11). I know this is strong language, but I have found no evidence in Scripture to support the conclusion that God loves every person in the same way. While it is often said, 'God loves the sinner, but hates his sin,' the psalmist says of God, 'You hate all workers of iniquity' (Ps. 5:5). It took the reconciliation of Christ's death to turn away God's hatred.

If I asked you, 'Do you love everybody in the world?', you would probably say 'Yes'. But I can make a reasonable guess that if you were to describe to me your love for your spouse (assuming you have one), the meaning of that word 'love' would deepen. If you love people you don't even know as much as you love your husband or wife, I can foresee problems for your marriage! Only the elect were *known* and loved by God before creation (Rom. 8:29). God 'sends rain on the just and on the unjust' (Matt. 5:45), but '[brings] about justice for his elect' (Luke 18:7, NASB). As Creator, God cares for the temporal lives of his creatures, but as Husband, Jesus Christ favours only his bride with sacrificial, eternal love (Eph. 5:25). A father might care about all children of the world, but that care does not even compare with his concern and love for his own children. So too, Christ died for 'the children of God ... scattered abroad' (John 11:52).

But doesn't this view limit God's love? On the contrary! it intensifies God's love, by limiting it only to those who believe. Such a love is far deeper than the indiscriminate, general benevolence we seem to be hearing much about today.

9.
Satisfaction guaranteed

For some reason, I tend to fall for products that advertise, 'Satisfaction guaranteed.' I like to know that what I'm getting is going to work; that is, after all, why I buy it.

Jesus Christ died to satisfy the just demands of a holy God. The prophet Isaiah said of the coming Messiah, 'He shall see his seed [the result of his work] ... and be satisfied' (Isa. 53:10-11). But did our Saviour *really* satisfy the wrath of God on behalf of all for whom he died?

In our last chapter we explored the purpose and extent of the work of Christ. In this chapter we will extend our discussion of Christ's 'mission accomplished' by viewing the cross from the aspect of *what* he accomplished rather than for whom he accomplished it.

All of us, by nature, know that God is angry with us. As a matter of natural revelation we learn that all people in every tribe and nation are at odds with God. Even pagan religions have appeasing of the gods at the centre of their beliefs and practices. Even though we as Christians sometimes try to reassure people that 'God loves you and Christ died for you,' they know that things are just not that simple. Things are not right, and if we are not reconciled with God, the picture is not as bright as we would have people believe.

Many people will pay for their sins in hell. Why, if Christ died for everybody to satisfy the wrath of God? The Princeton theologian of the nineteenth century, Benjamin B. Warfield, said of believers who do not accept the absolute, saving efficacy of Christ's work (by applying it even to those who will never believe): 'They necessarily turn away from a substitutionary atonement altogether. Christ did not die in the sinner's stead, it seems, to bear his penalties and purchase for him eternal life; he died rather to make the salvation of sinners possible, to open the way of salvation to sinners, to remove all the obstacles in the way of salvation. But what obstacle stands in the way of salvation besides the sinner's sin? And if this obstacle (their sin) is removed, are they not saved?'[1]

In fact, one evangelical writer says of those of us who hold the view of definite atonement: 'They also believe that the work of Christ on the cross was effective in and of itself.'[2] Indeed, we do believe that. Although it is absolutely essential that we trust Christ and accept his sacrifice for our sins, no one for whom Christ died will reject him. Christ's mission was accomplished!

I have frequently wondered, just for the sake of enquiry, 'What if the Bible taught that Christ died for every individual?' My conclusion was that I would be driven into the arms of universal salvation, not the middle view. That is because the Bible does not say Christ made redemption, reconciliation, propitiation, or anything else possible. He secured it for all for whom he died. Because the Bible allows for only a *saving* atonement every person would in that case be saved — whether a believer or not — because Christ had removed all charges. Let's look briefly then at the nature of the atonement.

Redemption

'To redeem' means 'to buy back', to 'return to one's possession by payment of a price'. You were kidnapped and held hostage by sin. But if you are a believer, Christ paid the ransom price for you to be freed so that you could become his possession. What kind of redemption do we have if most of the captives remain in captivity even after the ransom has been paid? The dictionary further defines redemption as 'purchasing a slave with a view to his freedom'. How could Christ purchase every person 'with a view to his freedom' if he knew all along that most would ultimately not be freed? This is brought out in Isaiah 53:10-11: 'He shall see his seed [the fruit of his work] and be satisfied.' How could Christ see people for whom he died in everlasting torment and 'be satisfied'? As Charles Spurgeon said, 'If it was Christ's intention to redeem all men, how deplorably has he been disappointed!'

Propitiation

Propitiation refers to the breaking away of the enmity and hostility that keep God at odds with us. Propitiation removes God's wrath. Yet people will be condemned for ever because they are still at odds with God. Jesus said, 'He who does not believe the Son shall not see life, but the wrath of God abides on him' (John 3:36). God cannot wait to unleash his wrath on the 'vessels of wrath' (Rom. 9:22). If Christ did not 'propitiate' God's wrath for me any more than he did for Judas Iscariot, how can I be sure that God is not going to consume me with his wrath? Someone might say, 'Because you believed.' But if that is what makes the difference it means that I, and not Christ, propitiated God's wrath.

Reconciliation

To 'reconcile' means 'to render no longer opposed'. Yet, people are assigned to hell for eternity because they are, and for ever will be, 'opposed' by God and to God. People who are reconciled are made friends. Jesus said he would lay down his life 'for his friends' (John 15:13). But will those who finally reject Christ be friends of God? Does God send his friends to hell? 'Depart from me, you cursed, into the everlasting fire' (Matt. 25:41). That is a far cry from friendship. The Bible says nothing of potential reconciliation, or a mere provision for reconciliation. Rather, it promises: 'Having been reconciled, we shall be saved' (Rom. 5:10). To be reconciled, then, is to be saved.

Substitution

The concept of substitution is found throughout Scripture as the act of one who suffers vicariously, or in the place of another. We read that Christ's blood is linked to 'the new covenant, which is shed for many for the remission of sins' (Matt. 26:28). Suppose a criminal was in the condemned cell, awaiting execution. A stranger goes to see the judge, and the judge agrees to accept the execution of this stranger (who is himself innocent) in the place of the real criminal. This person becomes the criminal's substitute. Then, suppose that after executing the substitute criminal, the judge then executes the real criminal too. The judge would be guilty of at least one murder. You were the criminal, but Christ stepped in and took your punishment. Because he took your punishment, you will not have to take it. God will not condemn both the Redeemer and the redeemed. This fact is an incentive to be numbered with the redeemed by trusting in Jesus Christ.

Sacrifice and satisfaction

Did Jesus satisfy God's justice on the cross? Or do we satisfy God's justice when we believe? If your answer is, 'At the cross,' then you believe that everyone for whom Christ died is cleared of all charges before God. If your answer is, 'When we believe,' we may ask, who is the real saviour? The Scriptures do not teach any such theory of self-satisfaction. We do not appease God's wrath by believing.

Then many of us, I'm sure, do not think God needs to be satisfied any more. Although there may at times be things that God doesn't quite like, he is, on the whole, nice to us, we think, so there's no reason to be afraid of him.

In the Old Testament, animal sacrifices were offered to prefigure the ultimate sacrifice of God's Son. Unlike the pagans who sacrificed, and in some places continue to sacrifice, in order to appease the gods, we have no way of appeasing our God. He must appease himself, by giving his own sacrifice. 'Now where there is remission of these [sins], there is no longer an offering for sin' (Heb. 10:18). If you are a believer, your sins have been remitted and no further sacrificial offering is needed to satisfy God. If, however, you are not a believer and you persist in unbelief until death, there has been no remission of your sins and the holy God still requires a sacrifice. That sacrifice will involve your spending eternity in hell, outside God's covenant of redemption.

One common response that the world makes to the idea of a sovereign God is that 'It's not fair for Christ to die for one person and not another'. But the same argument answers the atonement of the Son as the election of the Father. Have we forgotten what grace is all about? Is it wrong for people who don't deserve anything not to receive anything? What the fallen, alienated sinner needs to hear is not, 'God loves everybody, so if you're a "body" then God loves you.' No, the sinner needs more than that. He or she needs that intense love from all eternity that would mark out him or her. The sinner needs a passionate love, a committed love, a compelling love, which only comes in a discriminating, particular, selective relationship. Unconditional love is a love that is not based on the creature but the Creator.

Ambrose, an early church father, said, 'If you die in unbelief, Christ did not die for you.' Don't think *that* didn't make people think twice about the offer of Christ! We can hold out to the person who is at the end of his or her rope a redemption that is already complete, rather than a redemption that must be completed by believing. What this despairing world needs is not a hypothetical saviour, but a real one. They don't need a 'husband' who lets people with whom he is in love go to hell. And they need not worry that he will: 'Husbands, love your wives, just as Christ also loved the church and gave himself for it' (Eph. 5:25).

The same Bible that tells us that Christ gave 'his life a ransom for many' (Matt. 20:28; 26:28; Isa. 53:12; Heb. 9.28) also beckons, 'Come to Me, all you who labour' (Matt. 11:28); 'If anyone thirsts, let him come' (John 7:37). But whoever does not come was never included in God's redemptive programme anyway. And after all, isn't that what believing in Christ is all about?

The great Baptist evangelist, Charles Spurgeon, once said,
'And then I hear another objection —

'"How can you, sir, upon that theory, go to preach the gospel unto every creature?"

'I could not go upon any other theory, for I dare not go on that fool's errand of preaching a redemption that might not redeem ... a salvation that might not save. I could not go to a man and say, "Believe and thou shalt be saved."

'He would ask me, "Do you think *you* are going to be in heaven?"

'"Yes."

'"Why?"

'"Because Christ died for me."

'"But he died for everybody, so my chances are therefore just as good as yours."

'And after he had accepted my declaration, he might reply, "Is there any real reason why I should rejoice? Some for whom Christ died are in hell. What makes me so sure I will not go there? It is rather a faulty piece of good news, because it is nothing positive; it is a grand uncertainty you have proclaimed to me."'

Spurgeon concludes with the proper attitude towards this doctrine and the gospel message: 'If you believe on the Lord Jesus Christ, you shall be saved; if you do not, you shall be lost, and lost for ever. You are not redeemed — you are not saved — there is no salvation or redemption for you.'

Why should unbelievers get excited when I tell them, 'God loves you; Christ died for you'? Christ could have died for them; God could have loved them, but what good does that do them in hell if they reject the gospel?

We all know the sweet-talking romantic. He tells the girl how much he loves her and quotes some spine-tingling Shakespeare until she is putty in his hands. Then the girl comes to her senses and responds, 'I'll bet you say that to all the girls.' Later, she comes walking up to the house to pay a surprise visit to her silver-tongued Don Juan and overhears him speaking softly to another girl, with whom he doesn't even have a relationship, repeating the same rehearsed lines! Does that make her feel special — loved intimately and particularly?

What is the significance of telling a person, 'God loves you; Christ died for you,' if so many millions of these people whom God supposedly loves and died to save are condemned? If, however, we show an unbeliever that God loves *sinners* and Christ died for *sinners*, we have proof that this love and sacrificial death work. Those whom the Saviour loved and for whom he gave his life *are saved*! That's a love that works!

This doctrine sets before the unbeliever the availability and also the urgency of trusting in Christ. The person to whom we are witnessing is not potentially saved; he or she is actually lost. Rejecting Christ places a person outside the boundaries of redemption and God's eternal love.

You may ask, 'Is God loving when he chooses not to redeem everyone?' And I reply with my own question: 'Is God loving when he sends a person to hell — even after Jesus has already paid the price for his release?'

Incidentally, nobody will ever be able to say, 'Well, I looked for redemption, but there was nothing for me.' Christ obtained salvation for all who would, by the grace of the Holy Spirit, believe. The only people who will have no redemption will be those who never really looked. 'Seek, and you will find' (Matt. 7:7) is the promise of Scripture. If you are looking for redemption, it is because God is working in you. He is not far from you. Accept the sacrifice of his Son as full satisfaction of God's just and holy demands on you. Having trusted in Christ, you can be confident that 'There is therefore now no condemnation to those who are in Christ Jesus' (Rom. 8:1). Are you 'in him'? (see Eph. 1:4, 7, 13).

> Jesus paid it all,
> All to him I owe;
> Sin had left a crimson stain —
> He washed it white as snow.

God's grace works! Just as it worked at the cross in sealing and securing your redemption, it works when the Holy Spirit invades your life and transforms you with his powerful love. This is the Holy Spirit's act in this drama of redemption. When he draws people to himself and creates new life within them, neither circumstances, the devil, nor even death can keep God's eternal love from conquering us.

Imagine the joy of a husband and wife as they come to the end of the adoption process and can now take their new son or daughter into their home as a member of their family. The process began when the parents selected the child from among other children. Then there was the contract — the financial stage. The fees had to be paid, and outstanding debts had to be handled. And now, finally, the child is notified about his or her new family. After certain steps were taken, the child has a home. The child can feel secure and loved, part of a real family now.

God also takes a number of steps in securing our adoption into his family, namely the things he has done to give us new life.

1. Resurrection

Because we are 'dead in trespasses and sins' (Eph. 2:1), we need to be given new life. That process requires a resurrection, and it must come from a source outside ourselves.

When Jesus told his disciples that Lazarus had 'fallen asleep', they responded, 'Then he'll recover.' 'Then Jesus said to them plainly, "Lazarus is dead"' (John 11:11-14). And you know the rest of the story: Jesus went to the tomb and brought Lazarus back from the dead. This act was a preview of things to come. Not long afterwards, Christ was crucified and rose again. And because he lives, we are promised new life.

We are dead and unresponsive to the gospel in our natural condition. 'But he'll recover', we are so often told today. 'Just give him time.' But God says of men and women, 'They are dead.' Just as Jesus' words to his disciples were that Lazarus could not, and would not, recover, he convinces us elsewhere in Scripture that our spiritual condition is just as final, that we 'are all under sin' (Rom. 3:9).

Jesus told the multitude, 'You are of your father the devil, and the desires of your father you want to do' (John 8:44). You can't separate a person's will from his or her nature; and a nature that is opposed to God cannot and will not make a decision for God. Jesus said, 'Whoever commits sin is a slave of sin' (John 8:34). This, he said, is why 'You must be born again' (John 3:5-7).

We hear a lot about being 'born again', especially in America, where the media refers frequently to the 'born-again' constituency. At a time when even editors of pornographic magazines can claim to be born again, for our own good we must understand what it means to be born again.

First of all, the word translated 'again' should more accurately be rendered 'from above'. The new birth is *from above*, not from within. We do not cause or initiate regeneration. We are not born again because we believe. We believe because God reaches down from heaven and grants us the new birth.

You see, in our first birth, we entered our world in the family of Adam. Hence the psalmist lamented, 'Behold, I was brought forth in iniquity, and in sin my mother conceived me' (Ps. 51:5). We are 'by nature children of wrath' (Eph. 2:3). Our natural state is to reject God and do our own thing. This immediately rules out any possibility of our bringing about a change ourselves or even of our contributing towards obtaining this new birth.

Why is this? 'Those who are in the flesh [i.e. still have the old nature] cannot please God' (Rom. 8:8). Jesus said, 'Nor can a bad tree bear good fruit' (Matt. 7:18). A person's nature must be changed before his or her behaviour will change. The old person must be replaced by the new.

We had about as much to do with our new birth as Lazarus had to do with his physical resurrection. Again, our Lord says, 'No one can [even] come to me unless the Father who sent me draws him; and I will raise him up at the last day' (John 6:44).

We shall never know, I suppose — at least not until we see our Lord — why God did not just turn and walk away and leave us in our plight. God had warned Adam: 'You shall surely die' (Gen. 2:17). Adam refused to believe God, as we still do today; but still God's grace and mercy prevail.

2. Predestination

If you have been in the church for some time, you may have heard this popular illustration: 'God has cast his vote for your soul; Satan has cast his; now it's up to you to cast the deciding ballot.' I am convinced that if our Master was on earth today, he would respond to us as he did to his first disciples: 'You did not choose me, but I chose you' (John 15:16). I am afraid that we come perilously close to blasphemy in our exaltation of the human will, when we set it over and above (or at least on a par with) the will of God. If our decision determines whether God or Satan wins the great battle for souls, we are in serious trouble.

Since I have discussed predestination and election elsewhere in this book, I will not dwell on it extensively here. Let me say simply that J. B. Phillips is right: our god today is far too small. One evangelical scholar writes, 'Indeed, God would save all men if he could... God will achieve the greatest number in heaven that he possibly can. He does not love just some men; He loves all and will do everything within His loving power to save all He can... God will save the greatest number of people that is actually achievable without violating their free choice.'[3]

The marvellous truth is that because God has selected the recipients of his grace and placed them in Christ, he will also do all that is necessary, not only to make it possible for them to return to him but to make sure that they do!

'Whom he predestined, these he also called.' 'And as many as had been been appointed to eternal life believed' (Rom. 8:30; Acts 13:48). That is how much God thinks of you!

3. Redemption

The work of our Saviour was the payment of the ransom price that set us free in so far as judgement and condemnation are concerned. When we are born again we begin to actually experience this freedom secured by the Saviour.

We might think of this in terms of the construction of a building. The Father is the architect, the Son purchases the materials and the land and the Holy Spirit takes the Father's design and the Son's materials and constructs this magnificent cathedral of grace — the body of Christ.

Christ's death not only removed the penalty of sin; he endured the penalty of sin in our place. In the mystery of union or identification with Christ, he trampled death by death, and we were hanging there with Christ, on the cross. So, Paul says, 'If we have been united together in the likeness of his death, certainly we also shall be in the likeness of his resurrection, knowing this, that our old man was crucified with him, that the body of sin might be done away with, that we should no longer be slaves of sin' (Rom. 6:5-6).

Everything we lost in the Fall, Jesus Christ purchased back for us by his death. He crucified our old human nature that we had inherited from Adam, buried our old identity as 'in Adam' and bought for us a new life, a new identity. When the Holy Spirit comes to us, he re-creates our soul (see Eph. 4:24; Col. 3:10). We let go of our old identity and affirm the new. Christ spoke of our losing our life, our natural identity, so we can discover real life and a supernatural identity.

The same Christ who created the world, and then redeemed it, now comes to us as the one who re-creates us: 'For it is the God who commanded light to shine out of darkness who has shone in our hearts to give the light of the knowledge of the glory of God in the face of Jesus Christ' (2 Cor. 4:6).

The great expositor A. W. Tozer took the work of Christ on the cross seriously: 'All unannounced and mostly undetected there has come in modern times a new cross into popular evangelical circles ... This new evangelism employs the same language as the old, but its content is not the same and its emphasis is not as before ... The new cross does not slay the sinner; it redirects him. It gears him into a cleaner and holier way of living and saves his self-respect. To the self-assertive it says, "Come and assert yourself for Christ." To the egotist it says, "Come and do your boasting in the Lord." To the thrill-seeker it says, "Come and enjoy the thrill of the abundant Christian life."'[4]

The fact that we were 'bought with a price' (1 Cor. 7:23) means that we have become the property of someone else. At the cross, then, we were freed from slavery to sin — not to become 'in control' again, but to become the property of Jesus Christ, who frees us from other allegiances to be entirely his.

4. Glorification

The dictionary defines 'to glorify' as 'to magnify; to treat as more splendid or excellent than would normally be considered; brilliantly beautiful or magnificent'. *Glorification* is a state or condition of exaltation. From the Greek word for 'glory' we get our word 'doxology'. So then, to glorify someone is to dignify, honour and esteem that person.

Jesus said, 'Whoever exalts himself will be abased, and he who humbles himself will be exalted' (Luke 14:11). When we are united with Christ and become identified with his nature by humbling ourselves in recognition of our dependence upon him, we are exalted to the very heavens where Christ is seated in glory. But first we must recant from all the claims we used to hold to esteem, dignity and glory apart from God. Humiliation gives way to glorification.

So, the death of Christ corresponds to our redemption; his resurrection corresponds to our spiritual resurrection, as well as the judicial act of justification; and the ascension of Christ to the right hand of the Father corresponds to our glorification. That means that when Jesus died, we died; and when he rose from the dead, we also were given a fresh start, a new identity and a living spirit. Then, when the Saviour ascended, we too were exalted and glorified with him in heaven's courts. We, therefore, exist at present and into eternity as glorified persons.

Artists used to illustrate this truth by painting a golden halo above the head of a saint. Glorification is the consummation of salvation, the grand finale.

Hebrews 6:20 says, 'Jesus has entered as a forerunner for us, having become a high priest for ever according to the order of Melchizedek' (NASB). That means that Jesus pioneered the route we are going to travel. He was not the only one to ascend to the place of honour — just the first!

Because Jesus returned in victory to the Father, he has guaranteed our entrance into God's presence. When the disciple Stephen was being stoned to death, he 'being full of the Holy Spirit, gazed into heaven and saw the glory of God, and Jesus standing at the right hand of God' (Acts 7:55). Stephen could die in peace, knowing that Jesus was standing in his defence, prepared to crown him with the same glory he had seen in the vision.

One of my all-time favourite films is *Eddie and the Cruisers*, a rock-and-roll film about a group that had lost its leader, Eddie, in a road accident. One night Eddie took his girlfriend to a certain scrapyard. He hadn't been back to the scrapyard since he was a child. While sitting on the steps of the entrance, Eddie was telling his girlfriend about how he used to watch its elderly owner gradually transform the scrapyard into a festival of lights and creative structures. 'That old man actually thought he could make a castle out of junk,' Eddie reminisced. Just then he turned on the light and the entire yard became the 'castle' he had remembered in his earlier years. I thought as I heard those lines: '"That old man actually thought he could make a castle out of junk." That sounds like God!'

One popular poster in the USA is a picture of a child saying, 'I'm somebody, 'cause God don't make no junk.' Well, that's true! God doesn't make junk. He makes castles. So let's start seeing ourselves that way!

The Holy Spirit and human response

One question often asked in discussing God's sovereign activity in our lives is, 'Does God drag people into heaven kicking and screaming, against their will?' Far from it. God changes their will and their disposition. 'No one can come to me unless the Father who sent me draws him' (John 6:44), so his nature must be changed.

Try drinking water from a rusty cup. The water is not rusty; the cup is. No matter what kind of drink you might put in the cup, the rusty taste will still be there. The problem with us is not simply that we cannot make the right decision for Christ; instead it is that we possess a nature that is opposed to God. We reject Christ of our own free will. And if we accept Christ, it will be because God has changed our nature so that our will responds naturally and freely to God's grace.

We cannot separate a person's will from his or her nature. If it is a coyote's nature to howl, its instincts will lead it every so often to a particular rock where it will unleash its morbid call. But a rabbit will not howl; nor will a groundhog, for it is not their nature. Jeremiah said of humans, 'The heart is … desperately wicked; who can know it?' (Jer. 17:9). If an unbeliever rejects Christ, he or she is only responding as his or her nature dictates. If someone accepts Christ, his or her nature has been transformed. But in either case, it is the person's own will and decision making the choice.

The real question, then, is whether our choice is the determining factor in our salvation. I would answer, yes and no. Yes, if you do not choose Christ, you will be damned. If you do choose Christ, you will live. But the answer is also no, in the sense that only a move of God's grace can change your nature so that you will say yes to him. The human heart, untouched and unrenewed by God's effective grace, will never move a person towards the truth.

Regeneration is irresistible only because the God who regenerates is irresistible. Our natural blindness keeps our eyes from recognizing God's captivating features. So, when God heals our sight what can we say but, 'Now I see!'?

God's part/our part

We often speak of salvation in terms of 'God's part and our part'. However, this approach might suggest that we do, in fact, contribute to our own salvation.

I remember hearing the kind criticism of a man who said, 'Be careful, son; you almost make it sound like we don't have any part in salvation.'

'Almost?' I responded. 'I meant to go all the way!'

Why must we insist on having something to do with God's gift? Why can't we just say, 'To God alone be glory' — and really mean it? Any reference at all to 'our part' immediately tends to make for a salvation by works, not grace; that would mean that salvation was a joint work on the part of human beings and God, rather than the work of God alone. Even our decision does not merit eternal life.

But, you know, that is often the way we look at it. We agree perhaps that various 'works' such as being good to our neighbour and going to church every Sunday will not deserve eternal life for us; however, if we 'make a decision' and perhaps walk down an aisle or sign a card, or pray a 'sinner's prayer', we think then we shall attain eternal life.

On the contrary, when we respond in faith, we are in fact only reaching out for something that has already been accomplished by God. Our faith does not merit anything at all. Rather, it is our responsibility to embrace what God has done. Dr John R. W. Stott speaks to this: 'We must never think of salvation as a kind of transaction between God and us in which He contributes grace and we contribute faith. For we were dead and had to be quickened before we could believe. No, Christ's apostles clearly teach elsewhere that saving faith too is God's gracious gift.'[5]

The role of faith

An Orthodox priest was asked some time ago, 'Father, do you believe we are saved by faith or by works?'

'Neither,' the priest replied wisely, 'but by the mercy of God.'

We talk too much today about faith and not enough about the object of our faith. When we do that, faith becomes something subjective; it becomes an end rather than a means to the end, namely, Jesus Christ. Have you ever found yourself running around in circles, trying to keep the faith going? I know I have. The act of believing is not in itself the central issue. The one in whom the faith is placed is the source of our salvation, not faith itself.

Being justified by faith means that we are declared righteous because of what God has done, not because we have accepted what God has done.

Look at the following sentence and form an opinion about its truth or error: 'It is mine to be willing to believe; it is the part of God's grace to assist.' This slogan may appear harmless, and is, in fact, in line with what most of us have been taught. But the slogan's author and his teachings in this regard were condemned by more church councils than any other heretic or heresy in the history of the Christian religion. His name was Pelagius.

This distinction is important, as Martin Luther noted: 'If I know not the distinction between our working and the power of God, I know not God himself. Hence, I cannot worship him, praise him, or serve him; for I shall never know how much I ought to ascribe unto myself and unto God... No, the mercy of God alone does all things, and our own will does nothing; it is not active, but rather acted upon. And so it must be; otherwise the whole is not ascribed unto God.'[6]

We must, therefore, look to God even for the ability to trust in him. That is, after all, what faith is — depending completely on God.

Paul said, 'And do not be drunk with wine, in which is dissipation; but be filled with the Spirit' (Eph. 5:18). So we can assume that the influence of the Spirit in our lives can be compared to the way in which alcohol influences us. That being the case, let me use this illustration. By the time someone opens his seventh can of beer, his decisions are to a large extent being influenced by alcohol. We speak of 'driving while under the influence', and if the driver swerves and dodges other cars for excitement (doing things) he would not normally do when sober), he is still held responsible for his actions because, whether or not he was influenced by alcohol, his actions were the result of his own choices.

By nature, sin has intoxicated our whole being, and we cannot please God in any way. Nevertheless, our decision to turn from God is still our decision. Sin controls our faculties, but the decisions we make really are our own. When the Holy Spirit descends and intoxicates us with his new desires and power we just as naturally turn to God. Both the decision to turn from God and the decision to turn to God are really our decisions. But apart from God's grace (intoxicating grace) a decision for Christ is never going to happen.

The whosoever wills

'Come to Me, all you who labour and are heavy laden, and I will give you rest' (Matt. 11:28). That is an unqualified, bona fide offer from God to you and to every person who will come. There are no exceptions. God's electing, redeeming, calling grace does not exclude people from the invitation. Rather, God's grace includes people who would otherwise exclude themselves. In fact, this sovereign grace makes certain that the invitation will be successful, that people will respond. For 'No one can come to me unless the Father who sent me draws him' (John 6:44).

Why does God invite everybody to salvation if he knows that only the elect will come? First of all, it is through that general, universal invitation that the Holy Spirit reaches the elect with his Word and gospel. God has included you and me in the plan of missions and evangelism as agents and co-workers with him in bringing people to faith. Since you and I do not know who the elect are, we must simply cast our seeds upon the whole field and leave the results to God.

Also the universal invitation makes sure that when unbelievers stand before God on the judgement day, they will be without excuse. Nobody will be in heaven who did not choose to be there, and nobody will be in hell who did not choose estrangement from God. Everybody will get whatever he or she chose. It is not as if people wanted to come to God but are unable to do so. They do not want to come. The problem is not God's failure to speak, but rather our failure to hear and respond.

Dr. D. James Kennedy uses this illustration. He knows five men who are about to rob a bank. He tries to convince them not to commit the crime, but these men, evil-natured as they are, run for the bank, while Kennedy tackles one of the men and wrestles him to the ground. The others drive off to the bank. In the process, a guard is shot and the four robbers are sentenced to the electric chair. Can the one man whom Kennedy tackled say, 'I didn't go to the electric chair because I was better than the others'? Of course not. He was spared because Kennedy tackled him, not because his heart wasn't in the robbery. Dr Kennedy concludes, 'Those who go to hell have no one to blame but themselves. Those who go to heaven have no one to praise but Jesus Christ.'[7]

John Calvin said, 'We should be so minded as to wish all people to be saved,' I could not agree more. God said, 'I have no pleasure in the death of the wicked' (Ezek. 33:11). Neither should we.

When we make the general proclamation, 'Jesus Christ saves sinners,' the Spirit of God applies that and makes it relevant to particular individuals. This assures us that when we preach the gospel, God's Word 'shall not return to me void, but it shall accomplish what I please' (Isa. 55:11). That makes the evangelistic enterprise exciting! It really *is* fishing for people.

We learn from all this that even the application of salvation is God's gift. We look in vain for a peg upon which to hang our hat of conceit. The Spirit's calling grace is the 'straw that broke the camel's back'. And that camel's name is Pride.

Is it not marvellous that you can place your faith in someone who makes dead people live, who makes sinners into saints and who turns caterpillars into butterflies? Isn't it phenomenal that in a world of selfishness and shallow relationships, the Creator of the universe has taken such an interest in *you?*

Will Metzger writes, 'Our King is assured of a Kingdom and will neither be frustrated by human resistance nor obligated to save his creatures because of their supposed rights to his favour... The apostles were not preaching salvation by "making Christ your Saviour and Lord" in a good works fashion. He is already Lord; and therefore, our evangelistic call must be to come to Him as to the feet of a monarch, in submission to His person and authority.'[8]

Jesus Christ is your Lord, your Sovereign to whom you owe full allegiance. Will you do him homage? God's adventure with us has been in process from 'before the foundation of the world' (Eph. 1:4), and ours with him is about to begin. God's love has captured us and our lives will never be the same again.

10.
The buck stops here

Can you remember the last time you were spanked? I can well remember the last time it happened to me.

I was not in trouble so much for what I had done to the neighbour's cat as for what I did when I was confronted by my father. I actually challenged his authority. After all, here I was, fully fourteen years old. I knew I was mature because I was taking driving lessons! Besides, I was waiting for an opportunity like this to let my dad know I wasn't a child any longer.

I probably could have got off with a light warning that day, had I not dared dispute who was in charge. The cardinal sin of our family was for us children to call into question our father's jurisdiction over us. 'Boys will be boys,' Dad would occasionally say to Mother over a misdemeanour. But never were we to dispute his authority. The pain of having actually crossed that line was probably more emotionally intense than the physical discomfort experienced immediately following my brief encounter with autonomy.

Our human parents did not create us, of course. God did. And so God's authority extends over a greater realm in our lives because he is the source and origin of life itself. We must return to a belief something like 'God created you and has authority over your life,' instead of the many other options we presently have at our disposal. We submit because God's role as Creator is to rule, and our role as creatures is to be ruled.

Authority is one of the 'hot' issues of the day, in the church and in the world. At first thought we may fear it. Since the subject is of such crucial importance to our age, I want to take this chapter to address it.

A perennial problem

Of all God's creatures, we human beings are the meanest. We not only disobey our loving Creator, but we question the authority with which he governs our lives. Yet, out of our bitter rebellion, the angels thunder, 'The Lord is in his holy temple. Let all the earth keep silence before him' (Hab. 2:20).

We live during a period of a crisis of authority. 'We're not going to take it any more,' the crowd screams. To be ruled by anyone, or by anyone else's standards, beliefs, or convictions is viewed by our generation as moral weakness, not stability. The greatest problem in evangelical circles with regard to this issue, it seems, is inconsistent submission to God in all that he teaches and commands. We do not actually deny the authority of God outright. No, we know too well that to do so would be blasphemy. Rather, we ignore God's claims upon our lives when his reign encounters the rebel forces in our hearts.

People have always had a problem with God's authority — from Adam and Eve and Cain, on down the line to you and me. One notable example was Nebuchadnezzar, King of Babylon, who boasted, 'Is not this great Babylon, that I have built for a royal dwelling by my mighty power and for the honour of my majesty?'

At that very moment, in fact, 'While the word was still in the king's mouth, a voice fell from heaven.' That voice told Nebuchadnezzar that he had lost his kingdom and that he would wander like an animal, 'until you know that the Most High rules in the kingdom of men, and gives it to whomever he chooses'.

After his humiliation, the king responded,

> 'For his [God's] dominion is an everlasting
>   dominion ...
> All the inhabitants of the earth are reputed as
>   nothing;

He does according to his will in the army of
    heaven
and among the inhabitants of the earth.
No one can restrain his hand
Or say to him, "What have you done?"'
                                        (Dan. 4:30-35).

After he confessed, the king was given back his kingdom,
honour and dignity. 'Now I, Nebuchadnezzar, praise and
extol and honour the King of heaven, all of whose works are
truth, and his ways justice. And those who walk in pride he is
able to abase' (Dan. 4:37). King Nebuchadnezzar learned the
hard way that humility is the key to successful living under
God's reign.

God's authority extends over social, political and economic
affairs just as much as over our personal lives. We must not
limit God's authority. He is not the Lord of religion, but the
Lord of life. He is not merely concerned about governing our
moral or spiritual lives, but our total lives. As T. D. Price
said, 'Christianity is the least concerned about religion of any
of the world's faiths. It is primarily concerned about life.'

To suggest — even to a Christian audience — that the absolutes or universal laws of Scripture are to be applied to our
judicial, legal, cultural, social and economic institutions, as
well as religious, is apparently overstepping our bounds.
However, while separation of church and state may be toler-
able, separation of God and state is fatal to any civilization, as
the objective historian will attest.

God's sovereignty begins with individuals and ends with
the universe. To ignore this principle is to fly in the face of the
design of things. We are not talking about an allegiance to
outdated, old-fashioned morals and norms. Indeed, tradition
should no more be an absolute standard of reality than
fashion. No, our allegiance is to a guide that transcends even
time and space: 'Heaven and earth will pass away, but my
words will by no means pass away' (Matt. 24:35).

As Christians, we must insist — lovingly and respectfully,
to be sure — that God's authority over our private lives is
legitimate enough to rule our public lives as well. I have given
a good deal of thought to this, and have come to the conclusion that if I really do believe that God has spoken, and that
what he has spoken and commanded is true, then his words

are just as true for the governments of the nations as they are for me.

Because he cares

Authority implies dignity. I used to have a friend who smoked marijuana — and just about any inanimate object with leaves. He often tried to persuade me to smoke with him. We would stay out late, but at a certain time, I had to be home. He could not understand such strict measures as a curfew, and he thought my parents were really old-fashioned for not letting me smoke.

One night his parents and mine got together for the first time. At the dinner table, my friend's mother brought up the whole issue of parental authority. She called spanking 'beating' and insisted that parents who really loved their child would not impose their own morality. Later, my friend confided to me that by their lack of concern for where he was, what he was doing and when he would return, his parents were sending him the unintended signal: 'We do not care.' I had a curfew, not because my parents were power-hungry, but because they were concerned about me.

God imposes his moral expectations and universal laws on us because he has created the universe and, therefore, knows how it runs. He knows what is best for our lives. Obeying God's laws always works out to be in the best interests of both parties. God's interests and ours are the same. After all, we were created in God's image, bearing his concerns in a finite measure. Why then do we submit to God's authority over our lives? Because a loving God, who knows what is coming down the road, has commanded it. To live in discord with God is to live in discord with ourselves.

I would like to make one point. God's laws are not arbitrary. Sometimes we hear people say, 'Stealing is wrong simply because God says so. If God had said, "Blessed is he who steals," stealing would not have been a crime.' That simply is not true. Stealing is wrong because it is opposed to God's nature. God's laws are based on his very character; hence, no scriptural command is arbitrary and if you are obeying rules that cannot be morally linked to God's revealed attributes, you are not obeying God's rules. That is why God takes sin seriously: it goes against his nature.

When Christ appears, his authority will take the form of judgement. The Scriptures promise, 'For he must reign till he has put all enemies under his feet. The last enemy that will be destroyed is death' (1 Cor. 15:25-26).

The Son of God has been given the power and the authority to judge. Our response to Jesus Christ, therefore, is of urgent importance. We can beat our heads against the wall of the universe and scream in protest. Or we can submit to the one who designed and created the universe. If we dare to be instructed, he will teach us truth and give us life — because he is 'the way, the truth, and the life' (John 14:6).

As the 'kingdoms of men' (from Nebuchadnezzar's story) are under God's authority, so are the kingdoms of our hearts. Jesus said to the Father, 'You have given [me] *authority* over all flesh, that [I may] give eternal life to as many as you have given [me]' (John 17:2, italics mine). 'Is it not lawful for me to do what I wish with my own things?' asked Jesus (Matt. 20:15). 'As the clay is in the potter's hand, so are you in my hand' (Jer. 18:6).

It is time, I believe, that Christians began to spend more time studying the demands of Christ on us instead of our demands on Christ. For until we are convinced that Jesus Christ has the right and the power to reign over us, we shall never truly know his love and grace!

The authority of the Bible

We live in a world today where some people will try anything once — an age of experimentation, the testing of old forms and trying on of the new. In the 1990s most of those around us no longer believe that God has spoken. Hungry hearts are looking to false religious forms or, in many cases, no religious form at all. As Christians in the middle of this crisis, we are called to a new critical self-examination — asking ourselves if we have lost our conviction that God has really spoken, and spoken in such a way that it makes a difference in real life.

Oh, of course, we speak of God's Word, and we may actually believe that Word to be inerrant and infallible. But be careful: something can get lost in the transfer from creed to conscience, from policy to practice.

My word is an extension of myself. It tells you something about me. If my word is not credible or reliable, neither am I. In fact, Jesus once said that every word we speak comes from our hearts. God's living Word, Jesus Christ, and God's written Word, the Bible, have the same origins. When we know Christ, we know the Father. By knowing the living Word as revealed in the written Word we come to know the heart of God.

This book, the Bible, composes God's autobiography! 'A man is only as good as his word,' used to be a popular slogan. That is no less true of God than it is of us. If the Bible is not authoritative, then its Author also lacks authority and credibility.

Some in evangelical circles like to warn against raising the Bible to the divine level: 'The Bible isn't the fourth member of the Trinity,' they insist. And of course it isn't. Nevertheless, the Bible is an infallible witness to God and from God. There is nothing magical about reading Scripture. We do not become more spiritual simply by reading God's Word. It is not an end in itself. Rather, the Bible is a means to the end of discovering more about God and our relationship with him.

Two models

In a democracy, things are supposed to run by the 51% vote. The will of the people is the mood of the day. We begin to live our lives that way in the classroom, under peer pressure and in local elections. We learn the tendency to move with the majority, to 'do as the Romans do'. While retaining a measure of self-identity, many of us sacrifice our convictions at one time or another for the common cause of personal and social status. This is sometimes called 'the tyranny of the majority'.

How have we Christians been affected by this one-man, one-vote, standard of reality? For one thing, we tend to go in for pluralism. Were I to adopt a notion that goldfish had horns, I might well hear someone say, 'Well, plenty of good, Christian scholars are found on both sides of the horned goldfish debate, and I'm sure you can find biblical support for

both sides.' Whatever happened to the idea that there is only
one truth? Goldfish either do or do not have horns. The Bible
could not support both assertions — supposing that it dealt
with horned goldfish at all!

This is a respectable subjectivity *par excellence*. I can tell
another believer, 'You know, you and I are both right, even
though we maintain contrary positions,' and rarely be challenged. By saying 'Two plus two equals four', we rule out any
possibility of any other equation. In trying to cover up our dif-
ferences and bring together two opposing positions, we end
up with a contradiction without a conclusion.

Upon completing his 'Reformation' Symphony, Men-
delssohn was asked why he had prepared this tribute to the
Protestant Reformers. He replied, 'Because in those days
men had convictions; we moderns have opinions.' We have
lost so much of our conviction today. We too often take our
stand after carefully waiting and watching the world — putting our finger to the wind to test the direction. Then many
years after the world has taken its stand, we take ours — along
as popular lines as possible. We want to be fashionable, but
we end up fashionably late. I believe this is due to our having
more to do with trends and the rush of the crowd than with
'Thus saith the Lord'.

We often hear it said, 'Well, the Bible simply isn't all that
clear on that point,' when the scriptural position is staring
us in the face! To be sure, many things are not fully revealed;
but when the Bible speaks, it must be obeyed.

Another tendency of this method of interpreting reality is
the familiar cliché, 'We'll understand it better by-and-by,'
which really is only a spiritualized, sanctified way of saying
with the atheistic secularist, 'I can find no real, absolute truth
right here, right now.' That's frightening! We cannot ever
simply plead ignorance to something that has even the possibility of being revealed in Scripture. Ignoring God's teaching
in doctrine is just as arrogant as ignoring his instruction in
piety.

To the horned goldfish debate, the 'democratic disciple'
would respond, 'Well, that's your interpretation', as if it were
invalid simply because it is only my interpretation. Every
observation I make about life is my interpretation! That's
only obvious. But people who say this mean to legitimize the

existence of different positions. In other words, 'It's O.K. to have an interpretation; just don't say it's right!' That's what they mean. If I've never heard people preaching that goldfish have horns, I might discredit the hypothesis simply because, 'That's not what I've been taught.' These are symptoms of taking our democratic outlook into our relationship with God.

Similar to the 'democratic disciple' is the 'anarchist'. The 'anarchist' has a 'special line to God'. 'The Lord told me ...,' or 'The Lord spoke to my heart that ...' are giveaways of an anarchist. After all, when someone says, 'God told me ...,' who's going to argue?

Let's be honest. At least the secularists come out into the open and admit that they set their own standards; that they are their own god. Adrian Rogers said, 'It used to be "the Bible says"; today it has become, "well, it seems to me..."' The shape of truth does not change in response to how well it suits us. Sometimes we clash head-on with God as he reveals his will in his Scriptures. That is the crossroads of decision: how serious am I about the authority of God in my life?

Let me go back to a point mentioned earlier, pluralism (the existence of more than one point of view). There will always be different interpretations. No matter whether you are a historian, an archæologist, a biologist, or a theologian, every discipline has tension between a variety of concepts. However, when pluralism turns into eclecticism, which is actually selecting from a number of different systems, doctrines, or sources and blending the selections together, we appear more like bakers than believers. The 'democratic disciple's' recipe calls for a touch of this, a twist of that, swirled together with an additional pinch of something else. If I may be permitted the pun, this cake is half-baked! We do not pick and choose from systems, doctrines, or sources to suit our taste. We go straight to God's Word and allow it to build our system and dictate our doctrine. We need therefore to be on guard for our contributions to mix-and-match theology.

In contrast to a democracy, a monarchy is the rule of a king. It presupposes a kingdom, which in turn implies that there are citizens. Our King is the Lord Jesus Christ and as William Newton Clarke said, 'The kingdom of God is not a realm, but a reign; not domain, but dominion.'

John Calvin, the Genevan Reformer, said, 'Where God speaks, I speak; where he is silent, I must remain silent.' That is the response of a person committed to the monarchy of Jesus Christ. Because the Bible seems so often preoccupied with issues and matters that do not concern many of us today, we tend to try to twist God's arm to speak where there is no record, while silencing him on what we would boldly pronounce to be secondary issues.

We are not to be committed to the *status quo* or to an autonomous self-will; rather we must be constantly 'bringing every thought into captivity to the obedience of Christ' (2 Cor. 10:5).

Citizens of Christ's kingdom are law-abiding people. They obey the moral law of God as revealed in both Old and New Testaments. They keep Christ's commandments. They persist towards the goal of loving God with their whole being and caring for their neighbours. Of course, they fall short; but their loving King gives them strength to move on.

God has written the book and has issued his proclamation. The silence is broken by clarion trumpets. The command echoes across the hall: 'Hear him!'

The authority of the church

Ours is a culture that is always on the look-out for something new — a 'new improved' shampoo or a 'new formula' or a 'new style'. As the people of God, we are part of something very old.

The church began in the first century at Pentecost. At his ascension, Jesus told the disciples to wait for Pentecost, when the Holy Spirit would descend and inaugurate the new kingdom. One day, as disciples from various locations were gathered together 'in one place' (Acts 2:1), the Spirit did fall and the church was invested with supernatural power and authority.

Many people today are looking for a new Pentecost, as if the old one was not good enough to last through two millennia. As far as we know, only one Pentecost has occurred and will occur. We do not need another one. This event need not be repeated, but rather reinterpreted and recalled as the birth of a movement — the church of Jesus Christ — that continues to this day!

Pentecost was designed to empower the universal church with divine authority for its new mission. But we have neglected, ignored, or actually denied that authority. We need to recapture that historic continuity, the historic Spirit of the church. We have lost the tradition of church authority and in so doing have profoundly impoverished both ourselves and our age. It is in part because of this failure that the evangelical church in the West has failed to provide leadership in a declining civilization.

God invested his power, reputation and presence in this institution, the church. God is calling out a people from a mass of confusion and despair to form an eternal body of certainty and hope. The church is an authoritative institution; though the church, like individual Christians, often falls short in practice. When the church makes claims based on Scripture, those claims must be obeyed by the faithful.

In our day many evangelicals have rejected the authority of the church, a fact that I find distressing. Mind you, the church does not possess this authority on her own. And when the church speaks in a way that is contrary to the Word of God, she speaks with no authority at all.

One of the debates between the Protestant church and the churches with ancient continuity is over the issue of Scripture and tradition. Many evangelicals, for instance, are sceptical about classic tradition playing any definitive role in the life of the contemporary church. In fact, on a number of occasions I have gone through the themes presented in the other chapters of this book, referring occasionally to heroes of the faith who substantiate the historic continuity and antiquity of these truths. Often people will respond, 'It doesn't matter what the church has always believed and affirmed.' While the Bible is our only rule for faith and practice, the church — in its councils, creeds and confessions — assists us in interpreting the Scriptures responsibly. We are simply arrogant to suggest that we can come up with our own beliefs regardless of the historic stands made by the orthodox church down through the centuries, although those stands are always open to biblical censure.

The Bible and tradition are not at odds. Rather, they are

directly related. There is a sense in which it is true that the church is the mother of Scripture, since she gave birth to it. Sacred tradition communicated, documented and preserved the inspired message and inerrant text we now call the Bible. God was at work inspiring the early councils that placed the various books into the canon of Scripture just as sovereignly as he inspired the writers of the books.

Through the ages, through trials and tests of orthodoxy, through attacks and powerful arguments, the church has remained the pillar and support of Christian truth. This tradition reaches back to Abraham, through the wilderness, past the shadow of Sinai, through the prophets and up to Christ, who revealed the truths we as Christians hold central to our faith. And the early councils gave us our clear definition of the Trinity, the full divinity and humanity of Christ, and so on.

At a time when many believe the church has bartered her treasures from the vaults for the temporal benefits of fashionability, we vitally need to return to a strong, proud view of the church and its role in the world. The Nicene Creed states, 'I believe in one holy catholic and apostolic Church.' Do we believe that today?

The Enlightenment philosopher Voltaire said, 'In one century, Christianity will be dead.' Today, a century later, a Bible society operates out of his former home! Is it just an irony of history, or a promise fulfilled? 'I will build my church,' said the Lord Jesus Christ' 'and the gates of Hades shall not prevail against it' (Matt. 16:18).

We must begin again to take this heavenly establishment as seriously as God does. We must recognize and recapture the vision of Pentecost if we are to carry the church with us into the twenty-first century as the powerful, living witness to Jesus Christ. For the world at its worst needs the church at its best.

11.
Being righteous, not rigid

The renowned pollster George Gallup Jr set out to discover the religious climate and sympathies of the American people. He published his findings in *Search for America's Faith*.[1]

At first sight the results appear encouraging: up to sixty million born-again, evangelical Christians in America alone! That calls for celebration! But just as my pulse rate climbs and my excitement over the findings is at its peak, I am suddenly overwhelmed with disappointment. Talk about mixed emotions! How on earth could disappointment steal the thunder from these surprising findings? Precisely because it takes sixty million born-again Christians to make such a miserably low impact on American society and, in fact, on Western civilization!

Where in the world are these sixty million 'lights of the world'? Apparently we have a surplus in our nation of tasteless salt. We were promised in the last generation that if we talked to everyone we could and asked them to pray and accept Christ, society would improve. We did that. And people seemed to respond. But society grew markedly worse.

As I attend major Christian conventions — some of which are covered by international press organizations — I am awed by their size and scale. Christian programming is pumped over the airwaves just as fast as it can be produced, and Christian books abound. I had a chance to discuss this paradox with *60 Minutes* commentator, Morley Safer, at one such convention. In his television report, Safer surmised that during his entire ministry Jesus probably spoke to no more than 30,000 people. We've seen more people at one football game! Yet

Christ's message was powerful enough to turn the tide of history, even from a purely secular perspective.

Ninety-five per cent of all Americans profess a belief in God. Eighty per cent believe that God has a plan for their lives, while seventy per cent believe that the Bible is the inspired Word of God and that Jesus Christ is the divine Son of God! Those figures, read by sociologists in other countries, indicate that America is indeed a Christian nation, an orthodox, fundamentalist, Bible-believing Christian nation! But sociologists within our borders know better. Regardless of the impressive statistics, Christian faith not only maintains little influence in society generally; it claims little influence in the lives of its alleged adherents!

Pat Robertson laments that, according to Gallup, 'Only a fraction of the born-again Christians can name the authors of the four Gospels, or quote even a majority of the Ten Commandments.' What's more, 'The majority of born-again evangelicals in the U.S. define success as the acquisition of position and material wealth.'[2] The record is simply appalling. One fact that the Gallup polls uncovered was that there is not much difference in theology, convictions, or beliefs between the churched and the unchurched.

We who pride ourselves on our dedication and Bible-believing spirit apparently are not only accommodating the growth of a pagan, heathen culture; we are helping build it! We are its patrons, its consumers and often its architects.

Read the following description and determine whether the same characteristics of the world here can be applied to the problem areas in the church today: 'In the last days perilous times will come: For men will be lovers of themselves, lovers of money, boasters, proud, blasphemers [preachers of the health, wealth and happiness gospel], disobedient to parents, unthankful [taking God's grace for granted], unholy [no different from the ungodly with regard to essential values], unloving, unforgiving, slanderers, without self-control, brutal, despisers of good, traitors, headstrong, haughty [with a divisive, self-righteous piety], lovers of pleasure rather than lovers of God [asking, 'how God can please me?' — rather than the other way round], having a form of godliness [appearing very religious and 'separated'] but denying its power [ungodly at heart though perhaps pious] ... always learning and never able to come to the knowledge of truth' (2 Tim. 3:1, 7).

We have Bible conferences in our churches, on the mountains, in the cities and on cruise ships. We have audio cassettes, video cassettes, films, TV and radio, magazines, books, Bible colleges and seminaries, seminars and crusades. Suffice it to say that we are 'always learning' — but we are running low on the 'coming to a knowledge of truth' part. We may be able to recite John 3:16 and the four spiritual laws and interpret the meaning of the four-headed monster in Daniel's vision. But how deeply are we really affected by the teachings of Scripture?

Now that we have painted the sober picture of the lack of radical holiness among Christians generally, let's assess more practically our own allegiance to the lordship of Jesus Christ in his church.

Mirror, mirror on the wall

James has a lot to say about 'hearers versus doers'. He says that the hearer who is not a doer is like someone who is constantly looking in the mirror, absorbed with his or her own spirituality. 'How am I doing? Does my halo need recharging?' Hearers who are not doers are insecure, needing to feel pious, because they aren't. They know all the clichés and slogans. They know when to bow their heads and when to say something inspirational. But below the surface, they really are no different from those who do not even hear, much less do.

Godliness or piety

That word 'piety' has been around for a long time. A pious person is usually one who is deeply devoted to the duties and practices of the faith. In the purest sense piety is a characteristic necessarily belonging to every Christian. We must be devoted to the practical outworking of our faith.

However, the use of the word 'piety' has changed a bit since the late seventeenth century. The Pietist movement grew initially as a reaction of many Lutherans to the feeling that their faith was becoming cold and secular. They needed to warm up their zeal and the outward manifestations of their service for God.

Unfortunately, this movement that began with noble intentions became legalistic, moralistic and at times cultic. How quickly they forgot Luther's warnings against setting up a human standard of righteousness! The Pietists did not want to feed the mind so much as to temper the outward affections.

Most evangelicals or conservative Christians in the U.S.A are heirs of the Pietists, since their influence dominated so much of the development of the American church. The founders of Pietism wrote tracts and manuals designed to lead believers into a deeper walk with God. But the human, shallow rituals became as binding a faith as that against which the Reformers had rebelled. Today, we know more about steps to God than we know about God. We are more acquainted with the methods of getting closer to Christ than we are with him. This is the Pietist legacy.

With that historical background, we can see how easily our perception of holiness can be distorted. The Pharisees could well have been good Pietists. They followed their cues, knew the right methods, and at least appeared deeply spiritual — to the point that they delighted in saying so to others.

'If anyone among you thinks he is religious [pious], and does not bridle his tongue but deceives his own heart, this one's religion is useless. Pure and undefiled religion before God and the Father is this: to visit orphans and widows in their trouble, and to keep oneself unspotted from the world' (James 1:26-27).

Even if we can name the books of the Bible in order, there is no merit in that unless that same Bible leads us to help people all around us who cross our path daily. Real religion is for real life.

Now godliness is an entirely different subject. We have numerous calls to godliness in the Scriptures. Godliness is a fruit of the Spirit. Closely related to the term 'godly' is the word 'holy'. 'Holy' means 'set apart from the rest'. While Pietism would define holiness as being physically separated from the world and opposed to participating in its forms of entertainment, business and so on, biblical holiness goes much deeper. It is much more profound and demands much from us. What is the difference?

One commercial advertising a financial brokerage company claims to be 'a breed apart'. What that company is saying is this: 'Among all the companies that handle finances and real estate, we are separated from the rest.' Now, does that mean that this particular company is not part of the financial or business community? Is that what being 'a breed apart' means? Of course not. This company is distinct. It stands out among its competitors, but is not removed from them.

Christians are 'a breed apart'. They are not of this world, but they are in it. One of the problems Israel kept having in Egypt was that Israel began to lose her distinctiveness. Though in Egyptian captivity, the Hebrews were not, on the whole, treated poorly. Unfortunately, many people of Israel began to lose their identity. They became too Egyptian.

Egypt is used as a type or symbol of the world in the New Testament, as Israel is the shadow of the church. In his wisdom and good pleasure, God has not chosen to take us out of Egypt (the world); in a sense, we are strangers in a land that is not ours. But we are to retain and demonstrate our unusual, distinctive characteristics among those in the world with whom we come into contact. We participate in normal 'Egyptian' life in so far as it does not conflict with the laws and traditions of our fathers, as revealed in Scripture.

Holiness, then, is not adherence to a strict code of conduct. Godliness is not a matter of separation in the sense of self-righteous removal from society. Rather, these attributes manifest a heart and mind that are at peace with God and tenaciously committed to his lordly rule over their lives.

We are talking about reaching out in service to others and doing concrete things (works, if you will) that mean something — not to earn 'Brownie points' or to get closer to God, but as a natural manifestation of a heart converted by God's grace.

Saviour but not Lord?

A growing sentiment — and in fact, theological conviction — in some evangelical circles, teaches that it is possible for Jesus to be someone's Saviour without also being his or her Lord. In other words, a person can be saved even though he or she is unwilling to bow in humility and submission to Jesus Christ. I remember in my church how the pastor would follow up the invitation with the call: 'Many of you have made Jesus your Saviour, but you have never made him your Lord. You know heaven is your home, but you are not letting Jesus reign over you. Now is the time to make that commitment.'

My response today to those past experiences is twofold. First, we do not make Jesus either Saviour or Lord. He *is* Saviour; that is why I am saved. And he *is* Lord. Even if I refuse his gracious offer and go to hell, he is still Lord. In fact, Jesus' lordship is demonstrated by his ultimate triumph — whether I am in heaven or in hell. Second, if you have not confessed Jesus as Lord, heaven is not your home and Jesus is not your Saviour: 'If you [will] confess with your mouth the *Lord* Jesus and believe in your heart that God has raised him from the dead, you will be saved' (Rom. 10:9, italics mine).

Of course, just because we acknowledge the lordship of Christ over us and simply because we have confessed him as our King does not automatically mean that we will obey his orders at every turn. We do occasionally go our own way — and not without punishment. But we would never consider removing ourselves from the reign of Christ. Jesus Christ is not only our Priest; he is our Prophet and King — and not merely 'the coming King', but the presently reigning King. The 'Saviour but not Lord' teaching falls seriously short of the fulness of the faith, and its undergirding philosophy is destructive to our progress towards conformity to Christ's image.

Let go and let God

I am a native of California. That, I suppose, makes me an expert on being 'laid back'. If anybody has been brought up in an easy-going environment, I have. I have to admit that my theology has been warped by that philosophy as I, and many other Christians, have translated it into more spiritual terms, such as 'Let go and let God'.

Closely related to 'Let go and let God', is the slogan 'Let the Spirit lead.' Although we must not exclude the promptings of the Spirit, we must beware of baptizing our culture's 'If it feels good, do it' philosophy in sanctified clichés. As Christians, we are not fatalists. We do not believe — for the Scriptures do not teach — that 'What will be, will be.'

One of the biggest potential stumbling-blocks in our growth and maturity in Christ is the attitude that suggests we can sit back, let the Spirit have his way with us and, presto, we are victorious Christians. In the first place, we are not called into passivity. Nor do we 'let God', or 'let the Spirit' do anything. God does whatever he pleases. 'It is God who works in you both to will and to do for his good pleasure' (Phil. 2:13).

Instead, we must actively search the Scriptures to discover the demands and expectations that God has already revealed. We have clear laws and direct guidelines for daily living. We are not to sit back and wait for a spiritual wind from heaven. We are simply to apply to ourselves, accept and follow the teachings of Scripture.

We must stop making excuses for our disobedience. We are not disobedient because the devil makes us do it, nor because the flesh is just too powerful, nor because we are not sufficiently 'filled with the Spirit'. We are disobedient because we put our authority, desires and plans before God's interests. In other words, we do not follow our orders.

The process of sanctification, which is really the name of the theological theme we have been discussing, can best be defined by one word: obedience. 'Obedience' isn't a difficult word to understand, but it requires courage to apply it to everyday situations.

We live a life of grace. Only by grace are we saved; furthermore, it is only by grace that we perform good works. Grace and works are friends, not foes. Grace, in fact, can be said to be the mother of works. Grace undergirds the whole process from conversion to glorification.

We must not be afraid of taking the bull by the horns and being aggressive with life, with our emotions, our affections, our self-wills and our stubborn hearts. We can take charge in the power of Christ, asking God for his grace as we faithfully execute his plan for our lives. 'Work out your own salvation with fear and trembling' — that is our call to obedience — 'for it is God who works in you both to will and to do for his good pleasure' (Phil. 2:12-13) — that is the source.

12.
One thing left to do

My grandmother was the queen of making preserves. She was known throughout the community for the quality of her products. I remember well sitting on a stool in the kitchen and, like an obnoxious cat, watching her every move as she made her famous goods.

I would ask, 'Bigmama [we never called her 'grandma'], why are you always melting that wax over the fruit?' I didn't understand how wax could make any positive contribution to the flavour.

She answered, 'The wax seals the jar tightly so the fruit can't be contaminated. If I didn't seal it, the fruit would eventually rot.'

As an amateur in the preserving business, I saw as important the picking, purchasing and bottling stages. But I saw little importance in the sealing of the preserves.

You and I are God's preserves. What good would it do for God to choose us, redeem us and call us into union with his Son if he did not have a plan for preserving us as heirs of the eternal kingdom?

'In him you also trusted, after you heard the word of truth, the gospel of your salvation; in whom also, having believed, you were sealed with the Holy Spirit of promise, who is the guarantee of our inheritance until the redemption of the purchased possession, to the praise of his glory' (Eph. 1:13-14).

Christendom is not entirely at one on this matter of the security of the Christian. I must also concede that many of those who have espoused this doctrine have been guilty of taking God's grace for granted. Even though they might not come right out and state it, often people will live in such a way as to say, 'I made my decision. Jesus is my Saviour, and all my sins — past, present and future — are forgiven and forgotten. So I don't have to deal any more with those moments of weakness.' Professor Robert Godfrey once rather sarcastically caricatured this tendency by saying, 'God loves to forgive; I love to sin, so that makes for a good relationship.' That is *not* what God's sealing is all about.

A slogan that's best avoided

Some who believe that Christians are eternally secure give their doctrine the slogan: 'Once saved, always saved.' That slogan is very misleading. The slogan suggests that once people have made a decision for Christ, they can then go off and do their own thing, fully confident that no matter what they do or how they live, they are 'safe and secure from all alarm'. That simply is not biblical.

Salvation, to be sure, is an event. In other words, at some point in your life, the Holy Spirit moves and creates new life in your soul. But salvation is more than that. The *event* is *justification*, when God declares us righteous on the basis of the righteousness of Christ. But salvation is also a *process* over time, of becoming righteous, and this is called '*sanctification*'.

Sanctification *is* the Christian life, the daily pursuit of God and the transformation of the heart, mind and will. Our priorities and our view of life are drastically altered, revolutionized and reversed. We did not co-operate in our justification, but we must co-operate with God in our sanctification.

Some Christians have the idea that they must sit back and let the Spirit do everything. But the process towards maturity in Christ is not based on a passive view of life. We are not to wait for the Holy Spirit to perform some supernatural transformation in our lives. We actively pursue holiness and Christ-centredness in our lives, recognizing that the same one who commands us to work, persevere and obey also gives us the supernatural ability to do so. Just get on and do it! *You* do the work; but recognize that, if the work is done, it is *God* who has done it in and through you.

So then, when we speak of 'Once saved, always saved,' we are not taking into account the full scope of salvation. We have been saved (justification), we are being saved (sanctification), and we shall one day be saved (glorification). You cannot claim to have been 'saved' (justified) unless you are being sanctified. Jesus Christ is both Saviour and Lord.

Jesus made it plain throughout his ministry that someone could not become his disciple (and, therefore, could not receive eternal life) unless he or she was willing to 'take up his cross daily' and follow Jesus. The New Testament emphasizes denying yourself, dying to sin and deferring to others.

These terms identify a concept that is not in vogue today. At a time when even many church leaders are telling people to 'believe in yourself' and are preaching a gospel that is more concerned with fulfilling our desires than God's, we have difficulty in falling unreservedly into the arms of the Saviour in whom we find our only confidence. But of course, the gospel cannot ever be tailor-made to fit our self-serving expectations.

Cheap security

We touched earlier on another concept that contributes to our 'cheap grace' version of eternal security — the doctrine that says that many people have accepted Jesus Christ as their Saviour, yet have never accepted him as Lord. This two-stage conversion divorces Christ's work as Saviour from his position as Lord. It means that all we need to do is ask Christ to take away our punishment for sin; we do not have to demonstrate an interest in our removal from the power of that which stands between God and ourself.

Consider the rich young ruler who came to Jesus. He was willing to accept Jesus as Saviour: 'What good thing shall I do that I may have eternal life?' (Matt. 19:16). Instead of telling him, 'Now if you repeat this little prayer, you will be a child of God for ever,' Jesus demanded self-sacrifice to God in humble recognition of his position as Lord of the man's life. The ruler turned and walked away from the Saviour because he was not willing to bow to God's full lordship over himself and his possessions.

'Who then can be saved?' the disciples immediately asked

Jesus, who did not exactly run after the young ruler to beg him to reconsider.

Jesus answered, 'With men this is impossible, but with God all things are possible' (Matt. 19:26).

Any attempt to soften the blow of the gospel is erroneous and may well be responsible for deluding many souls that will be 'missing in action' when the final trumpet is sounded.

Martin Luther wrote, 'These things are to be openly proclaimed for the sake of the elect: that being by these means humbled and brought down to nothing, they might be saved.' 'The rest,' Luther says, 'resist this humiliation; nay, they condemn the teaching of self-desperation; they wish to have left a little something that they may do themselves.'[1]

Accepting Christ as Lord does not save us; but then, neither does accepting him as Saviour save us. Our acceptance does not change what Christ is. However, when God does save us and opens our eyes to him, the God we embrace is, and must be, both Saviour and Lord. And if God's lordship is not demonstrated in your life, you cannot presume that you are in fact 'safe and secure from all alarm'.

God is not running for the office of Lord. His is an established monarchy, not a democracy. Furthermore, we must rid our lives of this false concept of 'making Jesus more your Lord day by day'. We often speak as if the more we submit to Christ, the more power he has over us. God will never be more of a Lord over your life than he is right now. Christ is not in need of a change; we are.

The chain of salvation

Romans 8:30 makes clear what I like to call the chain of salvation, a chain whose links cannot be broken: 'Moreover whom he predestined, these he also called; whom he called, these he also justified; and whom he justified, these he also glorified.' Can someone be predestined, called, justified — and lost? This verse teaches us that when God starts something, he finishes it. Did you grant yourself salvation? Did you gain it yourself in the first instance? No, salvation was a gift. Remember, God justifies and condemns: 'Who shall bring a charge against God's elect? It is God who justifies. Who is he who condemns?' (Rom. 8:33-34).

Those whose hearts and minds have been (and are being) renewed by God's grace are not obsessed with worry about falling away because, although we shall always have periods of wandering around in the wilderness and falling into various temptations and sins, we really are becoming new persons. The ugly duckling is turning into a beautiful swan, to our surprise.

God never plants trees that do not bear fruit: 'You did not choose me, but I chose you and appointed you that you should go and bear fruit, and that your fruit should remain' (John 15:16). And the conclusion we can draw from James is, if you don't have the fruit, check the root!

Since God initially gives us the grace to believe in him and to turn from self, why would he not give us the grace to *keep on* trusting him? It simply isn't possible to believe in the possibility of losing salvation and in salvation by grace at the same time.

If we expect ourselves to maintain our faith and keep everything going, we fall under the reprimand of the apostle Paul, as he confronted the Galatian church: 'O foolish Galatians! Who has bewitched you? ... This only I want to learn from you: Did you receive the Spirit by the works of the law, or by the hearing of faith? Are you so foolish. Having begun in the Spirit, are you now being made perfect by the flesh [yourself]?' (Gal. 3:1-3).

We always approach God on his terms. Admittedly, this fact does serious injury to our pride, because it tells us that we are saved in spite of rather than because of ourselves.

What about free will?

Still another issue is involved as we see security in the light of the new birth or regeneration — the matter of free will.

'Nobody can take a believer out of Christ but the believer himself,' someone has said. However, God's Word tells us that '[No] created thing shall be able to separate us from the love of God which is in Christ Jesus our Lord' (Rom. 8:39).

That love of God which is 'in Christ' and for those who are 'in Christ' is much too powerful for that.

If we fit the description of a 'created thing', then even we cannot undo what God has done! If God loved us enough to choose us, purchase us with his Son's blood and bring us into union with himself, then it would be silly to wonder if God would keep on demonstrating his affection by preserving us in that love. Once God truly changes someone, that person never really wants to undo what God has done!

'Yes of course I was saved, but that was on Tuesday!' Many people see their salvation in terms of a decision they made. Since their assurance of salvation is based upon the shifting sands of human decision, they are faced with having to return frantically to the mirror every hour on the hour rather than resting in the character, plan and purpose of a sovereign God.

Think of the decisions you make every day. How about that decision to change employment or to move? Or what about your decision to go on that blind date the other night? What a disappointment that was! Wouldn't you fear having your eternal destiny hinging on your decision-making ability, an ability that might lead you one minute to commit yourself to a new course and to reject it the next? What a terrible way to live!

I am not playing down the necessity of making decisions, especially the one that concerns your eternal destiny. But it is reassuring to know that you can gauge your life by God's decision for you, and not the other way around. You can keep on going when you know that this is God's programme, God's project, and that God's interest in you creates within you an interest in him.

I remember how I used to ask Jesus into my heart as a child over and over again. Each time I intended to make absolutely certain that I was saved. Why do we do that? Why is it that in some churches we see the same people walking down the aisle week after week? Perhaps it is because we are looking to something *we* can do, or have done, to secure the kind of assurance we need. But we can't trust our feelings, our abilities of either will or effort; so we're left with having to trust in the ability of God, 'who is able to keep you from stumbling' (Jude 24).

We have the responsibility to 'go on to perfection' (Heb. 6:1). So we are responsible *to* persevere, but not *for* our perseverance. We are responsible *to be* saved, but not *for* our salvation.

To lose our salvation, we would have to return to a condition of spiritual death. What sort of author of regeneration would the Holy Spirit be if those whom he has resurrected and infused with eternal life were capable of dying to God again? 'Well, can't we commit spiritual suicide?' one might ask. Not if we take seriously the claim of 1 Peter 1:23 that we have been 'born again, not of corruptible seed but incorruptible'.

All in the family

If God really is our Father and we have been legally adopted by his design and will, then we are members of his eternal covenant family. We cannot erase our relationship with our heavenly Father, any more than we can erase our relationship with our earthly parents. Certainly I have fallen out of fellowship with my earthly parents, but it would be nonsense to say, 'I'm no longer your son; I hereby declare that you, Mother, did not give birth to me, and that you, Dad, are not my natural father.' That would be ridiculous.

Because we have been born into this royal family with an imperishable seed, we have been given the gift of perseverance to stand in the middle of frustration and despair and say, '[I am] confident of this very thing, that he who has begun a good work in [me] will complete it' (Phil. 1:6).

Earlier I said that one of the links in the chain of salvation is the fact that we are justified or declared righteous. That is an act. We also saw that the matter of being sanctified or made righteous is a process. We cannot see justification. Nor can we monitor justification, as we can, at least to a certain extent, sanctification. But we do believe God's Word that we are declared righteous even though we have some maturing to do.

In the matter of justification, we see a Judge; we picture a courtroom. In the matter of sanctification, we see a Father and the image of a home. I referred to the ugly duckling's becoming the beautiful swan. Sanctification involves that kind of transformation. Don't lose heart! If God started this work he will finish it!

A nation of sheep

Sheep do indeed stray from the shepherd. After all, if sheep did not tend to stray, why would they need a shepherd? But notice that the shepherd is always there to bring the sheep back.

Of course, we pay a penalty for straying. When we are living in a period of rebellion as children of God, life is 'hell on earth'. We may enjoy our brief moments of self-gratification, but the gains do not compare to the unrest and disappointment. 'How shall we who died to sin live any longer in it?' was the apostle Paul's question (Rom. 6:2). Living in rebellion against God goes against the grain for us now. We remember how exciting and pleasurable those former experiences used to be, but now they have lost their glamour. We are unhappy in sin, like a fish out of water, if our nature has truly been changed.

Backsliding can never be a crutch for having a fling. It is a very serious matter. 'Certain men have crept in unnoticed, who long ago were marked out for this condemnation, ungodly men, who turn the grace of our God into licentiousness' (Jude 4).

In the book of Hosea God called his people to repentance:

> 'Take words with you,
> And return to the Lord.
> Say to him,
> "Take away all iniquity;
> Receive us graciously,
> For we will offer the sacrifices of our lips" ...
> [And God said]
> "I will heal their backsliding
> I will love them freely,
> For my anger has turned away from[them]"'
> (Hosea 14:2, 4).

Backsliding is one thing; apostasy is yet another: 'They

went out from us [i.e. they abandoned the Christian fellowship — that's apostasy], but they were not of us; for if they had
been of us, they would have continued with us; but they went
out that they might be made manifest, that none of them were
of us' (1 John 2:19). John also says, 'Whoever transgresses
and does not abide in the doctrine of Christ does not have
God. He who abides in the doctrine of Christ has both the
Father and the Son' (2 John 9). And of Revelation 17:14, we
see that, with Christ in victory, 'Those who are with him are
called, chosen, and faithful.' Notice that it does not say, 'only
those of God's called and chosen who are faithful'. Rather, it
actually describes his followers as those who *are* 'called, chosen, and faithful'.

And, remember, even going through the motions of perseverance does not save us. When the Scriptures warn, 'He who
endures to the end shall be saved' (Matt. 24:13), it is still
God's perseverance with us that enables us to respond in
faithfulness to him.

The Christian faith flies in the face of social Darwinism and
its principles of perfection. Ours is not the 'survival of the fit-
test', but the 'survival of the weakest'. That is, only those who
come to terms with their spiritual impotency are granted the
grace of God to persevere in his strength. You will fall! Stop
trying to live the 'victorious Christian life' and simply live!

The Christian life cannot be described as 'three easy steps
to happiness'. As many who have been believers for some
time can testify, the Christian life is not easy, and it is not
always happy. The Christian life is a road that can be travelled
only by God's sovereign grace — a rough road, filled with
temptations and fears, rewards and failures, joys and frustrations. But we can take our eyes off the storm of our own
lives and look into God's face. Then we are reminded of
God's promise that all things are fitting into a pattern for our
good and his glory, that God is still in charge.

'If God is for us, who can be against us?' the apostle Paul
enthusiastically asked (Rom. 8:31). God is backing you in this
race of life, if you are on his team. He wants you to win over
the obstacles. God is shaping you into something of which he
can be proud. Your stubbornness, faithlessness, doubt and
self-will cannot stand in God's way. Indeed nothing 'shall be

able to separate us from the love of God which is in Christ Jesus' (Rom. 8:39).

> 'Now to him who is able to keep you from
>   stumbling,
> And to present you faultless
> Before the presence of his glory with
>   exceeding joy,
> To God our Saviour,
> Who alone is wise,
> Be glory and majesty,
> Dominion and power
> both now and for ever.
> Amen'

(Jude 24-25).

Appendix

Theologian Donald Bloesch has said, 'It's time for less dialogue, and more monologue — with God doing the talking!' When discussing doctrinal themes, many people say, 'It's just too confusing; it isn't really clear in Scripture.' But the confusion seems to be more appropriately charged to the account of the theological rhetoricians on both sides of the debate than to the Scriptures.

God has offered comment — at length — on the subjects raised in this book. To substantiate this, I now invite you to study closely a selection of passages related to the human condition, election, particular redemption, the new birth and security. After reading these passages, your faith will be strengthened. Though the listing is incomplete you may well be surprised to discover some new scriptural insights! After combing through some of the major passages that speak especially directly to the subject and consulting my copy of David Steele and Curtis Thomas's scriptural documentation, I was finally able to reduce the selection to its present form.

Not only does Scripture speak definitively in proclaiming God's electing grace; the historic, catholic, apostolic church affirms these truths as the truly orthodox position of the church of Jesus Christ. To substantiate this claim, I have also prepared an abbreviated historical sketch from church fathers to the present, including church creeds, showing how these all clearly affirm the doctrines of grace.

Let us join hands with the saints of the past and move into the future with God's Word and God's message for the present time.

The witness of Scripture

1. Adam, who represented our race before God and was the prototype of ourselves, was warned of the fatal consequences of eating from the tree of the knowledge of good and evil.

'In the day that you eat of it you shall surely die' (Gen. 2:16-17).

2. Because Adam chose disobedience and independence from God's restraints, he and our entire race committed spiritual suicide. Consequently everyone at birth is separated from God, without hope and with no potential within their grasp of believing the gospel or of loving God truly.

'What is man, that he could be pure? And he who is born of a woman, that he could be righteous?' (Job 15:14).

'Behold, I was brought forth in iniquity, and in sin my mother conceived me' (Ps. 51:5).

'The wicked are estranged from the womb; they go astray as soon as they are born' (Ps. 58:3).

'If you, Lord, should mark iniquities, O Lord, who could stand?' (Ps. 130:3).

'Who can say, "I have made my heart clean, I am pure from my sin"?' (Prov. 20:9).

'For there is not a just man on earth who does good and does not sin' (Eccles. 7:20).

'Truly, this only I have found: that God made man upright, but they have sought out many schemes' (Eccles. 7:21).

'The hearts of the sons of men are full of evil; madness is in their hearts while they live' (Eccles. 9:3).

'All we like sheep have gone astray; we have turned, every one, to his own way' (Isa. 53:6).

'We are all like an unclean thing, and all our righteousnesses are like filthy rags' (Isa. 64:6).

'The heart is deceitful above all things, and desperately wicked; who can know it?' (Jer. 17:9).

'For from within, out of the heart of men, proceed evil

thoughts, adulteries, fornications, murders, thefts, covetousness, wickedness, deceit, licentiousness, an evil eye, blasphemy, pride, foolishness. All these evil things come from within and defile a man' (Mark 7:21-23).

'Men loved darkness rather than light' (John 3:19).

'Jesus answered them, "Most assuredly, I say to you, whoever commits sin is a slave of sin"' (John 8:34).

'You are of your father the devil, and the desires of your father you want to do' (John 8:44).

'What then? Are we better than they? Not at all. For we have previously charged both Jews and Greeks that they are all under sin. As it is written:

"There is none righteous, no, not one;
There is none who understands;
There is none who seeks after God.
They have all gone out of the way;
They have together become unprofitable;
There is none who does good, no, not one"'

(Rom. 3:9-12).

'Therefore, just as through one man sin entered the world, and death through sin, and thus death spread to all men, because all sinned' (Rom. 5:12).

'You were slaves of sin' (Rom. 6:20).

'Because the carnal mind is enmity against God; for it is not subject to the law of God, nor indeed can be. So then, those who are in the flesh cannot please God' (Rom. 8:7-8).

'The natural man does not receive the things of the Spirit of God, for they are foolishness to him; nor can he know them, because they are spiritually discerned' (1 Cor. 12:14).

'You ... who were dead in trespasses and sins, in which you once walked according to the course of this world, according to the prince of the power of the air, the spirit who now works in the sons of disobedience, among whom also we all once conducted ourselves in the lusts of our flesh, fulfilling the desires of the flesh and of the mind, and were by nature children of wrath, just as the others' (Eph. 2:1-3).

3. Clearly our condition is so desperate that we can do nothing about it in our own power.

'Who can bring a clean thing out of an unclean? No one!' (Job 14:4).

'Can the Ethiopian change his skin or the leopard its spots? Then may you also do good who are accustomed to do evil' (Jer. 13:23).

'Nor can a bad tree bear good fruit' (Matt. 7:18).

'No one can come to me unless the Father who sent me draws him; and I will raise him up at the last day' (John 6:40).

'Not that we are sufficient of ourselves to think of anything as being from ourselves, but our sufficiency is from God' (2 Cor. 3:5).

4. Because of the shocking reality of human impotence, the initiative rests with God. We wait in the dark silence to hear God speak and deliver his decision. We expect nothing from God's hand but wrath and eternal hatred. But we are surprised that instead God decides (in fact, he has already decided from all eternity) to act in mercy and compassion by selecting a large number of people from every walk, every nation and tribe, every ethnic and racial background, to form a new race, establishing the Son as the new head, the second Adam, of this kingdom.

'Blessed is ... the people whom he has chosen as his own inheritance' (Ps. 33:12).

'Blessed is the man whom you choose, and cause to approach you, that he may dwell in your courts' (Ps. 65:4).

'Oh, ... that I may see the benefit of your chosen ones' (Ps. 106:5).

'Many are called, but few are chosen' (Matt. 22:14).

'And unless those days were shortened, no flesh would be saved; but for the elect's sake those days will be shortened... For false christs and false prophets will arise and show great signs and wonders, so as to deceive, if possible, even the elect... And he will send his angels with a great sound of a trumpet, and they will gather together his elect from the four winds' (Matt. 24:22, 24, 31).

'And shall God not avenge his own elect who cry out day and night to him?'(Luke 18:7).

'And we know that all things work together for good to those who love God, to those who are the called according to his purpose. For whom he foreknew [those with whom he had a prior relationship], he also predestined to be conformed to the image of his Son, that he might be the firstborn among many brethren. Moreover whom he predestined, these he also called; whom he called, these he also justified; and whom he justified, these he also glorified' (Rom. 8:28-30).

'Who shall bring a charge against God's elect?' (Rom. 8:33).

'Concerning the gospel they are enemies for your sake, but concerning the election they are beloved for the sake of the fathers' (Rom. 11:28).

'Therefore, as the elect of God, holy and beloved, put on tender mercies, kindness, humbleness of mind, meekness, longsuffering' (Col. 3:12).

'For God did not appoint us to wrath, but to obtain salvation through our Lord Jesus Christ' (1 Thess. 5:9).

'Paul, a servant of God and an apostle of Jesus Christ, according to the faith of God's elect' (Titus 1:1).

'To the pilgrims of the Dispersion ... elect according to the foreknowledge of God the Father, in sanctification of the Spirit, for obedience and sprinkling of the blood of Jesus Christ' (1 Peter 1:1-2).

'They stumble, being disobedient to the word, to which they also were appointed. But you are a chosen generation' (1 Peter 2:8-9).

'And those who are with him are called, chosen, and faithful' (Rev. 17:14).

5. God's choice is not based on anything in us — not even our decision to accept the gospel. After all, we accept the gospel only because God has accepted us in Christ through election. So our salvation is based on a decision made by God in eternity past, without respect to our personal choices or actions. Salvation is by grace alone.

'I will be gracious to whom I will be gracious, and — I will have compassion on whom I will have compassion' (Exod. 33:19; Rom. 9:15).

'Is it not lawful for me to do what I wish with my own things?' (Matt. 20:15).

'You did not choose me, but I chose you and appointed you that you should go and bear fruit, and that your fruit should remain' (John 15:16).

'And as many as had been appointed to eternal life believed' (Acts 13:48).

'(For the children [the twins: Jacob and Esau] not yet being born, nor having done any good or evil, that the purpose of God according to election might stand, not of works but of him who calls), it was said to her, "The older shall serve the younger." As it is written, "Jacob I have loved, but Esau I have hated." ... So then it is not of him who wills, nor of him who runs, but of God who shows mercy' (Rom. 9:11-13, 16).

'But indeed, O man, who are you to reply against God? Will the thing formed say to him who formed it, "Why have you made me like this?" Does not the potter have power over the clay, from the same lump to make one vessel for honour and another for dishonour? ... [He did so] that he might make known the riches of his glory on the vessels of mercy, which he had prepared beforehand for glory' (Rom. 9:20-21, 23).

'Even so then, at this present time there is a remnant according to the election of grace. And if by grace, then it is no longer of works; otherwise grace is no longer grace' (Rom. 11:56).

'What then? Israel has not obtained what it seeks; but the elect have obtained it, and the rest were hardened' (Rom. 11:7).

'Oh, the depth of the riches both of the wisdom and knowledge of God! How unsearchable are his judgements and his ways past finding out!

> "For who has known the mind of the Lord,
> Or who has become his counselor?"
> "Or who has first given to him
> And it shall be repaid to him?"
> For of him and through him and to him are all things, to
> whom be glory for ever. Amen'

(Rom. 11:33-36).

'God has chosen the foolish things ... God has chosen the weak things ... the things which are despised God has chosen ... that no flesh should glory in his presence' (1 Cor. 1:27-29).

'Just as he chose us in him before the foundation of the world, that we should be holy and without blame before him in love, having predestined us to adoption as sons by Jesus Christ to himself, according to the good pleasure of his will... In whom also we have obtained an inheritance, being pre-destined according to the purpose of him who works all things according to the counsel of his will, that we who first trusted in Christ should be to the praise of his glory' (Eph. 1:4-5, 11-12).

'Knowing, beloved brethren, your election by God. For our gospel did not come to you in word only, but also in power, and in the Holy Spirit and in much assurance' (1 Thess. 1:4-5).

'God from the beginning chose you for salvation by the Spirit and belief in the truth' (2 Thess. 2:13).

'Therefore I endure all things for the sake of the elect' (2 Tim. 2:10).

'Has not God chosen the poor of this world to be rich in faith and heirs of the kingdom?' (James 2:5).

'Therefore, brethren, be even more diligent to make your calling and election sure, for if you do these things you will never stumble; for so an entrance will be supplied to you abundantly into the everlasting kingdom of our Lord and Saviour Jesus Christ' (2 Peter 1:10).

'And all who dwell on the earth will worship him, whose names have not been written in the Book of Life of the Lamb slain from the foundation of the world' (Rev. 13:8).

6. Having marked us out for an eternal relationship before the world was ever created, the Father placed us 'in Christ'. Just before his crucifixion, Christ prayed, 'not ... for the world but for those whom you have given me, for they are yours' (John 17:9). The elect, fallen in sin, needed a Saviour to satisfy the righteous demands of God's justice. Jesus died as a sacrifice for the eternal family of God, securing everything necessary for eternal life and redemption. Christ's saving work, freely offered to all, guaranteed the salvation of the elect, clearing them from every charge against them.

The following verses establish the atonement as a saving work. Not only did Christ's work make salvation possible, nor is it merely the basis for redemption; it is redemption. And all for whom Christ died are, or will eventually be, saved.

'And you shall call his name Jesus, for he will save his people from their sins' (Matt. 1:21).

'Being justified freely by his grace through the redemption that is in Christ Jesus' (Rom. 3:24).

'But God demonstrates his own love toward us, in that while we were still sinners, Christ died for us. Much more then, having now been justified by his blood, we shall be saved from wrath through him' (Rom. 5:8-9).

'For if when we were enemies we were reconciled to God through the death of his Son, much more, having been reconciled, we shall be saved by his life' (Rom. 5:10). To be reconciled by Christ's death is in fact to be saved.

'Grace to you and peace from God the Father and our Lord Jesus Christ, who gave himself for our sins, that he might deliver us from this present evil age, according to the will of our God and Father' (Gal. 1:3-4).

'Christ has redeemed us from the curse of the law' (Gal. 3:13).

'And you, who once were alienated and enemies in your mind by wicked works, yet now he has reconciled in the body of his flesh through death, to present you holy and blameless and irreproachable in his sight' (Col. 1:21-22).

'Christ Jesus came into the world to save sinners' (1 Tim. 1:15).

'Who gave himself for us, that he might redeem us from every lawless deed and purify for himself his own special people zealous for good works' (Titus 2:14).

'Not with the blood of goats and calves, but with his own blood he entered the Holy Place once for all, having obtained eternal redemption' (Heb. 9:12).

'For Christ also suffered once for sins ... that he might bring us to God' (1 Peter 3:18).

7. *The Bible clearly states that Christ came to earth with a mission that involved a particular number of people. He came*

to fulfil the contractual agreement made within the Trinity from all eternity. Given to the Son by the Father, the elect alone are purchased at the cross.

'The Son of man did not come to be served but to serve, and to give his life a ransom for many' (Matt. 20:28).

'For this is my blood of the new covenant, which is shed for many for the remission of sins' (Matt. 26:28).

'But I said to you that you have seen me and yet do not believe. All that the Father gives me will come to me... For I have come down from heaven, not to do my own will, but the will of him who sent me. This is the will of the Father who sent me, that of all he has given me I should lose nothing, but should raise it up at the last day' (John 6:36-40).

'I am the good shepherd. The good shepherd gives his life for the sheep... I am the good shepherd; I know my sheep and am known by my own. As the Father knows me, even so I know the Father; and I lay down my life for the sheep... [The accusers said,] 'If you are the Christ, tell us plainly.' Jesus answered them, "I told you, and you do not believe ... because you are not of my sheep"' (John 10:11, 14-15, 24-26). Christ gives his life for the sheep, which does not include these particular unbelievers.

'"It is expedient for us that one man should die for the people, and not that the whole nation should perish." Now this he did not say on his own authority; but being high priest that year he prophesied that Jesus would die for the nation, and not for that nation only, but also that he would gather together in one the children of God who were scattered abroad' (John 11:50-53).

'Jesus spoke these words, lifted up his eyes to heaven, and said: "Father, the hour has come. Glorify your Son, that your Son also may glorify you, as you have given him authority over all flesh, that he should give eternal life to as many as you have given him... I have glorified you on the earth. I have finished the work which you have given me to do... I pray for them. I do not pray for the world but for those whom you have given me, for they are yours. And all mine are yours, and yours are mine, and I am glorified in them. Now I am no longer in the world, but these are in the world, and I come to you. Holy Father, keep through your name those whom you have given me, that they may be one as we are"' (John 17:1-2, 4, 9-11).

'Shepherd the church of God which he purchased with his own blood' (Acts 20:28).

'For as by one man's disobedience many were made sinners, so also by one man's obedience many will be made righteous' (Rom. 5:19).

'He who did not spare his own Son, but delivered him up for us all, how shall he not with him also freely give us all things? Who shall bring a charge against God's elect? It is God who justifies. Who is he who condemns?' (Rom. 8:32-34).

'Just as he chose us in him before the foundation of the world, that we should be holy and without blame before him in love... In him we have redemption through his blood, the forgiveness of sins, according to the riches of his grace' (Eph. 1:4-7).

'Husbands, love your wives, just as Christ also loved the church and gave himself for it, that he might sanctify and cleanse it with the washing of water by the word, that he might present it to himself a glorious church, not having spot or wrinkle or any such thing, but that it should be holy and without blemish' (Eph. 5:25-27).

'And for this reason he is the Mediator of the new covenant, by means of death, for the redemption of the transgressions under the first covenant, that those who are called may receive the promise of the eternal inheritance' (Heb. 9:15).

'Christ was offered once to bear the sins of many' (Heb. 9:28).

> 'You are worthy to take the scroll,
> And to open its seals;
> For you were slain,
> And have redeemed us to God by your blood
> Out of every tribe and tongue and people and
>   nation' (Rev. 5:9).

8. *Chosen in Christ, redeemed by Christ, and now brought into union with Christ, the people of God are born again —*

spiritually resurrected, given the gift of faith, justified and baptized into the church.

The following verses underline the reality that our new birth is the result of God's will and action, not ours. We are saved, not because we found Christ, but because he found us.

'I was sought by those who did not ask for me; I was found by those who did not seek me' (Isa. 65:1).

'Then I will give them one heart, and I will put a new spirit within them, and take the stony heart out of their flesh, and give them a heart of flesh' (Ezek. 11:19).

'And he said to me, "Son of man, can these bones live?" So I answered, "O Lord God, you know." Again he said to me, "Prophesy to these bones and say to them, 'O dry bones, hear the word of the Lord! Thus says the Lord God to these bones: "Surely I will cause breath to enter into you, and you shall live. I will put sinews on you and bring flesh upon you, cover you with skin and put breath in you; and you shall live. Then you shall know that I am the Lord."'" So I prophesied as I was commanded; and as I prophesied, there was a noise, and suddenly a rattling; and the bones came together, bone to bone... Then he said to me, "Prophesy to the breath, prophesy, son of man, and say to the breath, 'Thus says the Lord God: "Come from the four winds, O breath, and breathe on these slain, that they may live."'" So I prophesied as he commanded me, and breath came into them, and they lived, and stood upon their feet, an exceedingly great army' (Ezek. 37:3-9). This is, by the way, an excellent illustration of what happens when we share the gospel with people. We 'prophesy', that is, preach the message, and God causes the individual to respond.

> 'All the inhabitants of the earth are reputed as
>   nothing;
> He does according to his will in the army of
>   heaven
> And among the inhabitants of the earth.
> No one can restrain his hand
> Or say to him, "What have you done?"'
>
> (Dan. 4:35).

Take some time to read the entire chapter for deeper insight on this point.

'And the apostles said to the Lord, "Increase our faith"' (Luke 17:5).

'But as many as received him, to them he gave the right to become children of God, even to those who believe in his name: who were born, not of blood, nor of the will of the flesh, nor of the will of man, but of God' (John 1:12-13).

'Jesus answered and said to them, "This is the work of God, that you believe in him whom he sent... All that the Father gives me will come to me, and the one who comes to me I will by no means cast out... No one can come to me unless the Father who sent me draws him; and I will raise him up at the last day... It is the Spirit who gives life; the flesh profits nothing. The words that I speak to you are spirit, and they are life. But there are some of you who do not believe" ... And he said, "Therefore I have said to you that no one can come to me unless it has been granted to him by my Father." From that time many of his disciples went back and walked with him no more' (John 6:29, 37, 44, 63-66).

'Without me you can do nothing... You did not choose me, but I chose you... I chose you out of the world' (John 15:5, 16, 19).

'When they heard these things they became silent; and they glorified God, saying, "Then God has also granted to the Gentiles repentance to life"' (Acts 11:18).

'Now when the Gentiles heard this, they were glad and glorified the word of the Lord. And as many as had been appointed to eternal life believed' (Acts 13:48).

'Now a certain woman named Lydia heard us. She was a seller of purple from the city of Thyatira, who worshipped God. The Lord opened her heart to heed the things spoken by Paul' (Acts 16:14).

'Or do you despise the riches of his goodness, forbearance, and longsuffering, not knowing that the goodness of God leads you to repentance?' (Rom. 2:4).

'For he says to Moses, "I will have mercy on whomever I will have mercy, and I will have compassion on whomever I will have compassion." So then it is not of him who wills, nor of him who runs, but of God who shows mercy' (Rom. 9:15-16).

'Even so then, at this present time there is a remnant according to the election of grace. And if by grace, then it is no longer of works... What then? Israel has not obtained what it seeks; but the elect have obtained it, and the rest were hardened... For the gifts and the calling of God are irrevocable' (Rom. 11:5-7, 29).

'But the natural man does not receive the things of the Spirit of God, for they are foolishness to him; nor can he know them, because they are spiritually discerned' (1 Cor. 2:14).

'For who makes you differ from one another? And what do you have that you did not receive [from God]? Now if you did indeed receive it, why do you glory [boast] as if you had not received it?' (1 Cor. 4:7). Here Paul rebukes the pride of the Corinthians in thinking that their spiritual inheritance was inherently theirs, and forgetting that they didn't have anything that was not given to them as a gift from God.

'And we have such trust through Christ toward God. Not that we are sufficient of ourselves to think of anything as being from ourselves, but our sufficiency is from God' (2 Cor. 3:4-5).

'And what is the exceeding greatness of his power toward us who believe, according to the working of his mighty power' (Eph. 1:19). We believe by the working of God's power.

'And you he made alive, who were dead in trespasses and sins, in which you once walked according to the course of this world, according to the prince of the power of the air, the spirit who now works in the sons of disobedience, among whom also we all once conducted ourselves ... and were by nature children of wrath, just as the others. But God, who is rich in mercy, because of his great love with which he loved us, even when we were dead in trespasses, made us alive together with Christ (by grace you have been saved), and raised us up together, and made us sit together in the heavenly places in Christ Jesus, that in the ages to come he might show the exceeding riches of his grace and his kindness toward us in Christ Jesus. For by grace you have been saved through faith, and that not of yourselves; it is the gift of God, not of works, lest anyone should boast' (Eph. 2:1-9).

'For it is God who works in you both to will and to do for his good pleasure' (Phil. 2:13).

'If God perhaps will grant them repentance, so that they may know the truth' (2 Tim. 2:25).

'Of his own will he brought us forth by the word of truth' (James 1:18).

9. We all understand our bent towards independence and infidelity. If the security of our salvation depends on our ability to choose and hang on to Christ, we will be caught on the tread-mill of a self-centred works-righteousness. Once God starts something, he finishes it. A truly born-again person can do nothing to lose salvation; it is eternal. But we are responsible to persevere. If we do not, it is not because we have lost salvation, but because we never had it in the first place.

The following verses assure us of the security of our relation-ship with God in Christ.

> 'For the mountains shall depart
> And the hills be removed,
> But my kindness shall not depart from you,
> Nor shall my covenant of peace be removed,'
> says the Lord'
>
> (Isa. 54:10).

'I will make an everlasting covenant with them, that I will not turn away from doing them good; but I will put my fear in their hearts so that they will not depart from me' (Jer. 32:40).

'What do you think? If a man has a hundred sheep, and one of them goes astray, does he not leave the ninety-nine and go to the mountains to seek the one that is straying? And if he should find it, assuredly, I say to you, he rejoices more over that sheep than over the ninety-nine that did not go astray. Even so it is not the will of your Father who is in heaven that one of these little ones should perish.'

'For God so loved the world that he gave his only begotten Son, that whoever believes in him should not perish but have everlasting life' (John 3:16).

'He who believes in the Son has everlasting life' (John 3:36).

'Most assuredly, I say to you, he who hears my word and believes in him who sent me has everlasting life, and shall not come into judgement, but has passed from death into life'

(John 5:24). Once we are given eternal life, we are no longer in the position where we can ever again come into judgement.

'All that the Father gives me will come to me, and the one who comes to me I will by no means cast out... This is the will of the Father who sent me, that of all he has given me I should lose nothing, but should raise it up at the last day' (John 6:37, 39).

'My sheep hear my voice, and I know them, and they follow me. And I give them eternal life, and they shall never perish; neither shall anyone snatch them out of my hand. My Father, who has given them to me, is greater than all; and no one is able to snatch them out of my Father's hand' (John 10:27-30).

'Father, keep through your name those whom you have give me' (John 17:11).

'There is therefore now no condemnation to those who are in Christ Jesus' (Rom. 8:1).

'For whom he foreknew, he also predestined to be conformed to the image of his Son, that he might be the firstborn among many brethren. Moreover whom he predestined, these he also called; whom he called, these he also justified; and whom he justified, these [not just some of these] he also glorifed. What then shall we say to these things? If God is for us, who can be against us? ... Who shall bring a charge against God's elect? It is God who justifies. Who is he who condemns? ... Who shall separate us from the love of Christ? Shall tribulation, or distress, or persecution, or famine, or nakedness, or peril, or sword? ... In all these things we are more than conquerors through him who loved us. For I am persuaded that neither death nor life, nor angels nor principalities nor powers, nor things present nor things to come, nor height nor depth, nor any other created thing, shall be able to separate us from the love of God which is in Christ Jesus our Lord' (Rom. 8:29-39).

'Jesus Christ ... will also confirm you to the end, that you may be blameless in the day of our Lord Jesus Christ. God is faithful, by whom you were called' (1 Cor. 1:7-9).

'God is faithful, who will not allow you to be tempted beyond what you are able, but with the temptation will also make the way of escape, that you may be able to bear it' (1 Cor. 10:13).

'Having predestined us to adoption as sons by Jesus Christ

to himself, according to the good pleasure of his will... In him you also trusted, after you heard the word of truth, the gospel of your salvation; in whom also, having believed, you were sealed with the Holy Spirit of promise, who is the guarantee of our inheritance until the redemption of the purchased possession, to the praise of his glory' (Eph. 1:5, 13-14).

'The Lord will deliver me from every evil work and preserve me for his heavenly kingdom. To him be glory for ever and ever. Amen!' (2 Tim. 4:18).

'For by one offering he has perfected for ever those who are being sanctified' (Heb. 10:14).

'Therefore, since we are receiving a kingdom which cannot be shaken, let us have grace, by which we may serve God acceptably with reverence and godly fear' (Heb. 12:28).

'Blessed be the God and Father of our Lord Jesus Christ, who according to his abundant mercy has begotten us again to a living hope through the resurrection of Jesus Christ from the dead, to an inheritance incorruptible and undefiled and that does not fade away, reserved in heaven for you, who are kept by the power of God through faith for a salvation ready to be revealed in the last time' (1 Peter 1:3-5).

'They went out from us, but they were not of us; for if they had been of us, they would have continued with us; but they went out that they might be made manifest, that none of them were of us... And this is the promise that he has promised us — eternal life' (1 John 2:19, 25). When people apostasize, that is, repudiate the Christian faith and leave the church altogether, that is evidence that they were never Christians to begin with.

'For whatever is born of God overcomes the world. And this is the victory that has overcome the world — our faith... And this is the testimony: that God has given us eternal life, and this life is in his Son. He who has the Son has life... These things I have written to you who believe in the name of the Son of God, that you may know that you have eternal life... And we know that the Son of God has come and has given us an understanding, that we may know him who is true; and we are in him who is true, in his Son Jesus Christ. This is the true God and eternal life' (1 John 5:4, 11-13, 20).

'To those who are called, sanctified by God the Father, and preserved in Jesus Christ' (Jude 1).

> 'Now to him who is able to keep you from
>   stumbling
> And to present you faultless
> Before the presence of his glory with
>   exceeding joy,
> To God our Saviour,
> Who alone is wise,
> Be glory and majesty,
> Dominion and power,
> Both now and for ever.
> Amen'

(Jude 24-25).

The witness of the saints

The witness of the saints through the ages yields a forthright, dogmatic and dynamic testimony to the centrality of these truths in the life of the holy, apostolic, catholic church of Christ. Periods of intense impact coincide curiously with the periods in which these teachings are vigorously defended and faithfully proclaimed.

The following excerpts, though incomplete, should present a clear and definitive statement concerning the position of the church from early times to more recent history. Here, then, one finds not only an appeal from Scripture, but a decisive call from the historic church as well.

Human inability

Barnabas, the associate of Paul, said in A.D. 70, 'Learn: before we believed in God, the habitation of our heart was corrupt and weak.'

The celebrated church father, *Ignatius,* writing in A.D. 110, said, 'They that are carnal [unbelievers] cannot do the things that are spiritual... Nor can the unbelievers do the things of belief.' By this he meant that an unbeliever cannot do something that is entirely foreign to his or her nature. The reason people do not choose Christ is that, in their own natural state, they do not have the disposition or desire to be ruled by God.

Justin Martyr concurred strongly with this conviction when, in A.D. 150, he wrote, 'Mankind by Adam fell under death, and the deception of the serpent; we are born sinners... No good thing dwells in us... For neither by nature, nor by human understanding is it possible for men to acquire the knowledge of things so great and so divine, but by the energy of the Divine Spirit... Of ourselves it is impossible to enter the kingdom of God... He has convicted us of the impossibility of our nature to obtain life... Free will has destroyed us; we who were free are become slaves and for our sin are sold... Being pressed down by our sins, we cannot move upward toward God; we are like birds who have wings, but are unable to fly.'

'Like birds who have wings, but are unable to fly' — what a lucid metaphor Justin Martyr uses to paint the realistic if unfortunate picture of people's spiritual abilities! We have a will. If you reject Christ, you do it *willingly*. Nevertheless, your will is in bondage to sin and the selfish nature owned by each of us.

It is interesting that wings and flying have been used most frequently to convey the sensation of our spirit. *Clement of Alexandria* (A.D. 190) repeated the metaphor: 'The soul cannot rise nor fly, nor be lifted up above the things that are on high, without special grace.'

The earlier period of church history proved to be a challenging one. Spin-off heresies were abundant and one early father in particular, named *Origen*, was charged with such departure. Nevertheless, he was compelled to say with the broad consensus of early Christianity, 'Our free will ... or human nature is not sufficient to seek God in any manner.'

And in A.D. 330 an orthodox historian of the church said,

'The liberty of our will in choosing things that are good is destroyed.'

I have read a great deal about 'secular humanism', that is, the teaching that we have within ourselves whatever it takes to better ourselves and our world on our own — without God. This, far from being a recent development, is only a contemporary reappearance of the ancient heresy known to the church as Pelagianism.

The monk Pelagius taught that by nature humans are neither depraved nor good. We are neutral and our will is free to choose either to accept Christ and his gospel or reject it. Furthermore, he said that a Christian could lose favour and hence be lost if he or she failed to co-operate (do *his or her* part) with God in salvation. A modified and more moderate view, called appropriately 'semi-Pelagianism', arose and both movements were eventually uprooted by the Catholic Church and officially declared heretical in the ancient Council of Orange (to which you will find a detailed reference later on).

The person most responsible for calling the church to the defence of the gospel of God's free and omnipotent grace was *St Augustine*, hailed by Protestants and Roman Catholics alike as being the virtual founder of the Western church.

Here is just one of Augustine's many defences against the error, written in A.D. 370: 'If, therefore, they are servants of sin (2 Cor. 3:17), why do they boast of free will? ... O, man! Learn from the precept what you ought to do; learn from correction, that it is your own fault you have not the power ... Let human effort, which perished by Adam, here be silent, and let the grace of God reign by Jesus Christ ... What God promises, we ourselves do not through free will of human nature, but he himself does by grace within us ... Men labour to find in our own will something that is our own, and not God's; how they can find it, I know not.'

Though the church had taken a stand, men and women rather quickly began to forget this message, led more by the feelings and impressions of their human nature than by the Spirit of God. Hence began what were to be called the 'Dark Ages'. Flickers of light shone here and there — for instance, Anselm of Canterbury in the thirteenth century and the

Gottschalk renewal in the ninth. *Thomas Aquinas* brought these teachings back into scholarly debate and he was an able defender of this message, recalling the memory of Augustine.

But soon the church had become so corrupt both in doctrine and practice that it was virtually indistinguishable from the pagan world except in outward form, ritual and legalistic regulations. The errors condemned by the church in the fifth century were now the popular religion of the day, from peasant to pope.

Now we come to the sixteenth-century Reformation, one of the most profound movements in the tradition of the ancient gospel. The most luminous figure of the era, *Martin Luther*, was vehement in his defence of this gospel (A.D. 1530): 'A man without the Spirit of God does not do evil against his will, under pressure, as though he were taken by the scruff of the neck and dragged into it; no, he does it spontaneously and voluntarily... On the other hand, when God works in us, the will is changed under the sweet influence of the Spirit of God... With regard to God and in all that bears on salvation or damnation, man has not "free will", but is a captive, prisoner and bondslave.'

Unconditional election

Fortunately, the Scriptures do not leave us in the Garden of Eden, fallen, torn, twisted and ruined; neither does the gospel of the fathers of our faith. Faced with such a helpless and impotent condition, one must conclude that God will have to decide to do something about this mess if, in fact, he does anything at all (which he is not even remotely obligated to do). The Christian gospel refers to this decision of God as 'unconditional election'. We do not place ourselves in Christ when we choose him; rather, the Father placed us in Christ when he chose us before creation.

In A.D. 69, *Clement of Rome*, the same Clement mentioned in Paul's epistle to the Philippians (4:3), had this to say: 'Let us therefore approach him in holiness of soul, lifting up pure and undefiled hands unto him, with love towards our gentle and compassionate Father because he made us an elect portion unto himself... Seeing then that we are the special elect portion of a holy God, let us do all things that pertain unto holiness... There was given a declaration of blessedness upon them that have been elected by God through Jesus Christ our Lord... Jesus Christ is the hope of the elect.'

Again, Clement prayed, 'Creator, guard intact unto the end the number that hath been numbered of thine elect throughout the whole world, through your beloved Son Jesus Christ... For you chose the Lord Jesus Christ, and you chose us through him for a peculiar people.'

In a conversation with Trypho the Jew, Clement compared the election of the nation of Israel to the election of people from every nation to form a new spiritual nation: 'God, out of all nations, took your nation to himself, a nation unprofitable, disobedient and unfaithful; thereby pointing toward those that are chosen out of every nation to obey his will, by Christ, whom also he calls Jacob, and names Israel.'

To the Ephesians (the same local church to whom Paul sent his inspired epistle), *Ignatius*, (A.D. 110) wrote, 'To the predestined ones before all ages, that is, before the world began, united and elect in a true passion, by the eternal will of the Father...'

This was a common form of salutation in letters from the fathers of the church. Can you imagine how vigorously these teachings must have been taught and how excited the early Christians must have been about them, for the fathers' common letters to have been addressed to the churches in this manner?

The *Church of Smyrna* (mentioned in the book of Revelation) circulated a letter to the other churches reminding them of their commitment to the gospel (A.D. 157): 'It behoveth us to be very scrupulous and to assign to God the power over all things...'

Later in the letter, the Church of Smyrna refers to examples in which it would appear that evangelists of the church had been preaching to crowds and the people watching noticed that some responded so passionately and others violently rejected the message. Why do some choose Christ and others reject him? The Church of Smyrna writes further, 'The multitude marvelled that there should be so great a difference between the unbelievers and the elect... The Lord maketh election from his own servants... Glory be unto God for the salvation of his holy elect.'

Earlier I referred to *Justin Martyr's* discussions with Trypho the Jew. His evangelistic appeal to Trypho, using this doctrine of election as a common point of discussion, might give us a clue as to how we can effectively use this teaching in our message, particularly in speaking with Jews: 'In all these discourses I have brought all my proofs out of your own holy and prophetic writings, hoping that some of you may be found of the elect number which through the grace that comes from the Lord of Sabaoth, is left or reserved [set apart] for everlasting salvation.'

Let's turn now to a different sort of conversation — this time, a discussion between *Octavius* (a Christian) and *Coecilius* (a heathen). Coecilius charges that the Christian teaching of election is essentially no different from the pagan notion of fate: 'Whatsoever we [pagans] ascribe to fate, so you to God; and so men desire your sect not of their own free will, but as elect of God; wherefore you suppose an unjust judge, who punishes in men lot or fortune, and not on the basis of their will.'

Of course, Coecilius misunderstood the church's teaching on election. That is to be expected from a pagan. After all, look at how many Christians today would have the same misconception! Unfortunately, we do not have any record of Octavius' response to the charge.

However, *Irenæus*, the disciple of the martyr Polycarp (who was a disciple of the apostle John) said in A.D. 198, 'God hath completed the number which he before determined with himself, all those who are written, or ordained unto eternal life... Being predestinated indeed according to the love of the Father that we would belong to him for ever.'

And check to see if this description of the early church by Irenæus fits the contemporary scenario: "The tower of election being everywhere exalted and glorious.'

Clement of Alexandria, writing in A.D. 190, explains election to some extent and encourages those to whom he is writing in their own standing: 'Through faith the elect of God are saved. The generation of those who seek God is the elect nation, not the place [i.e., not an earthly, political nation] but the congregation of the elect, which I call the church... If every person had known the truth, they would all have leaped into the way, and there would have been no election... You are those who are chosen from among men and as those who are predestined from among men, and in his own time called, faithful and elect, those who before the foundation of the world are known intimately by God unto faith; that is, are appointed by him to faith, grow beyond babyhood.'

This concise statement resembles the declaration of Paul's former companion *Barnabas*, in A.D. 70: 'We are elected to hope, committed by God unto faith, appointed to salvation.'

Cyprian (A.D. 250) said, 'This is therefore the predestination which we faithfully and humbly preach.'
Can we say today that our churches are 'faithfully and humbly' preaching the glory of God in election?

Ambrose of Milan (A.D. 380) buttressed the beauty, grandeur and mystery of the church with this doctrine: 'In predestination the church of God has always existed.'

Today, many people will consent to the idea of God's having chosen them, but, to circumvent the humbling and intimidating impact of the real doctrine of election, they will invent their own. One of these responses is cased in the form of this argument: 'Yes, God chose me, but it's because he knew I would choose him.' You see, here you and I are still able to maintain that salvation is based on us — or something we did. Conditional election (God's choosing me because he knew I would choose him) is no election at all; it's nothing more than mere advanced knowledge of something that we would do of our own will and resources.
This argument is by no means new. Notice *Augustine's*

response (A.D. 380) and I think you will see what I mean: 'Here certainly, there is no place for the vain argument of those who defend the foreknowledge of God against the grace of God, and accordingly maintain that we were elected before the foundation of the world because God foreknew that we would be good, not that he himself would make us good. This is not the language of him who said, "Ye have not chosen me, but I have chosen you"' (John 15:16).

Earlier fathers had defended unconditional election against the 'vain argument' of foreseen faith. One such person was *Origen*, who, as noted earlier, was later (A.D. 230) to depart from the truth of Christianity: 'Foreknowledge is not the cause of things future... Not therefore anything will be because God knows it to be future, but because he has willed it to be future. He knows it to be so... Our election does not arise from works, but from the purpose of God, from the will of him that calleth.'

Many of us have heard of *William Tyndale*. John Hus, John Wycliffe and William Tyndale were the first Reformers of what would come to be called the Protestant Reformation. They were faithful Roman Catholics who nevertheless attacked the corrupt faith and practice of the church in their day. For this they were condemned by their church. These forerunners of the Reformation had much to say about election. For them and for the Reformers who would come later, this truth was the missing link that corrupted the whole chain of doctrine in the late medieval church: 'Now may not we ask why God chooseth one and not another; for God hath power over all of his creatures to do as he pleaseth' (Tyndale).

The Reformation was not a crusade against indulgences, papal infallibility, or rituals. These things only became issues as indulgences cheapened (and in fact replaced) the doctrine of grace, and the pope's infallibility was challenged only when he began to challenge the doctrines of sovereign grace. No, the real issue was that the church would simply not give in to Paul's affirmation: 'It is not of him who wills, nor of him who runs, but of God who shows mercy' (Rom. 9:16). *Martin*

Luther said, 'Although this matter is very hard for the "prudence [thinking] of the flesh," which is made even more indignant by it and brought even to the point of blasphemy, because here it is strangled to death and reduced to absolutely nothing, man understands that salvation comes in no way from something working in himself, but only from outside himself, namely, from God, who elects. But those who have the "prudence of the Spirit" delight in this subject with ineffable pleasure.'

Martin Luther's dialogue with Erasmus of Rotterdam (the church's defender against Luther) is well known. In it Luther commends Erasmus for at least being willing to discuss the issue of election. He found that nobody really wanted to talk about the subject. People just did not think the doctrine of election was all that important. Of course they didn't! After all, who wouldn't place a low value on a humbling doctrine of this nature? Luther said, 'I give you hearty praise on this, Erasmus — that you alone, in contrast with all others, have attacked the real thing, that is, the essential issue. You have not wearied me with those extraneous issues about the papacy, purgatory, indulgences and such like — trifles, rather than issues... You, and you alone, have seen the hinge on which everything turns, and aimed for the vital spot.'

Furthermore, according to Luther, 'There are two causes which require such things to be preached. The first is the humbling of our pride and knowledge of the grace of God. The second is the future of the Christian faith itself.'

Luther said that if 'God is thus robbed of his power to elect' he might as well take a vacation and go 'to an Ethiopian feast' since he would not be much of a God at all.

I will not even indulge in quoting excerpts from the other Reformers: Zwingli, Calvin, Bucer, Knox and others. Suffice it to say that the essence of the Reformation — its *raison d'être*, if you will, was at the heart a defence of this great truth of the gospel.

The 'prudence of the flesh' (as Luther would call it) again rolled onto the shores of history as fog dominates the early morning. The Pilgrims had brought this faith to America, but by the turn of the eighteenth century Deism and Semi-

Pelagianism had gained the ascendancy. This condition called for another great movement for the gospel of grace. This movement did come and many historians credit the impact of this event with the American Revolution. It was of course, the Great Awakening. Its leaders all held to these doctrines. In fact, its most acclaimed leader, *Jonathan Edwards*, wrote, 'From my childhood up, my mind had been full of objections to the doctrine of God's sovereignty, in choosing whom he would to eternal life; and rejecting whom he pleased ... But I have often, since that first conviction, had quite another kind of sense of God's sovereignty than I had then. I have often since had not only a conviction, but a *delightful* conviction. The doctrine has very often appeared exceedingly bright and sweet. Absolute sovereignty is what I love to ascribe to God ... And wherever the doctrines of God's sovereignty with regard to the salvation of sinners were preached, there with it God sent revival.'

Edwards was joined in his effort by the powerful English evangelist, *George Whitefield*. Whitefield and John Wesley had begun the movement that would come to be called Methodism. Eventually their theological convictions drew them into controversy, and Wesley cut himself off entirely from fellowship with Whitefield (an estrangement which Whitefield lamented the rest of his life). Yet even Wesley said of Whitefield, 'Have we read or heard of any person who called so many thousands, so many myriads of sinners to repentance?'

Whitefield preached the gospel to more people than any person of his day — thousands at one time without any modern amplification. He was asked by many of his Deistic friends (like Benjamin Franklin) why he made so much of election. He responded: 'This is one reason, among many others, why I admire the doctrine of election, and am convinced that it should have a place in the gospel ministry, and should be insisted on with great faithfulness and care... I shall only say, it is the doctrine of election that mostly presses me to abound in good works.

This makes me preach with comfort, because I know that my salvation does not depend upon my free will, but the Lord makes me willing in the day of his power; and can make use

of me to bring some of his elect home, when and where he
pleases.' 'When' God pleased was often, and 'where' he
pleased was right across Britain and America!

It is no accident that the greatest missionary heroes, such as
William Carey, Hudson Taylor, John Patton and David
Livingstone, were well-versed in, and passionately concerned
about, this truth. Evangelism takes on real meaning when we
are preaching 'the power of *God* unto salvation'. No better
example can one find of this principle in recent history than
the famous evangelist *Charles Haddon Spurgeon*, who said,
'Brethren, we must always believe this and preach it, for it is
the sum of all true doctrine. If you do not make salvation to
be wholly of the Lord, mark my word, you will have to clip
salvation down, and make it a small matter. I have always
desired to preach a great salvation, and I do not think that
any other is worth preaching... We cannot preach the gospel
unless we preach the electing, unchangeable, eternal,
immutable, conquering love of Jehovah.'

Definite atonement

The late professor of theology, Lewis Sperry Chafer,
reflected a popular view in evangelical circles with regard to
the death of Christ when he said, 'The death of Christ upon
the cross does not save anybody — either actually or potentially. It makes all men saveable.' If we are not convinced by
Scripture — the highest standard and only objective guide for
truth — it should be undeniable that the faith of our fathers
sharply condemns this popular denial of the power of the
cross.

When Jesus died for us, he paid the price for our sins; he
actually redeemed us and cleared us of all charges, taking
them upon himself. In short, he saved us. That is the message
of the gospel. Our Lord came with a mission: to redeem the
elect of God, not to make possible the redemption of every
person.

Once again we turn to Paul's partner in ministry, *Barnabas*,
who, in A.D. 70, spoke of Christ saying, 'I see that I shall thus
offer my flesh for the sins of the new people.'

Justin Martyr (A.D. 150) said, 'He endured the sufferings for those men whose souls are [actually] purified from all iniquity... As Jacob served Laban for the cattle that were spotted, and of various forms, so Christ served even to the cross for men of every kind, of many and various shapes, procuring them by his blood and the mystery of the cross.'

The Bible says that Christ died as 'a ransom for all' (1 Tim. 2:6). But 'all' does not always mean 'each and every individual', as can be proved from many other passages in which the word 'all' appears. Here is how the *Church of Smyrna* handled Christ's being 'the Saviour of the world' (A.D. 169): 'Christ suffered for the salvation of the whole world of them that are saved.'

And here is how *Irenæus* (A.D. 180) handled the 'all' of 1 Timothy: 'He came to save all, all, I say, who through him are born again unto God, infants and little ones and children and young men and old men.' In other words, Christ died not just for one particular kind of people, one special ethnic group or age, sex, or geographical area. He died for everybody — all nationalities and so on. Irenæus continued, 'Jesus is the Saviour of them that believe; but the Lord of them that believe not. Wherefore, Christ is introduced in the gospel promising to give his life a ransom, in the room of, many.'

Tertullian (A.D. 200) said plainly, 'Christ died for the salvation of his people ... for the church.'

In A.D. 250, *Cyprian* said, 'All the sheep which Christ hath sought up by his blood and sufferings are saved... Whosoever shall be found in the blood, and with the mark of Christ shall only escape... He redeemed the believers with the price of his own blood... Let him be afraid to die who is not reckoned to have any part in the cross and sufferings of Christ.'

In the year 320, *Lactantius* elaborated on this teaching: 'He was to suffer and be slain for the salvation of many people ... who having suffered death for us, hath made us heirs of the everlasting kingdom, having abdicated and disinherited the people of the Jews... He stretched out his hands in his passion and measured the world, that he might at that very time show that a large people, gathered out of all languages and tribes, should come under his wings, and receive the most great and sublime sign.'

In response to 'who gave himself up for us *all*', *Eusebius* replies (A.D. 330): 'To what "us" does he refer, unless to them that believe in him? For to them that do not believe in him he is the author of their fire and burning. The cause of Christ's coming is the redemption of those that were to be saved by him.'

Julius said, in A.D. 350, 'The Son of God, by the pouring out of his precious blood, redeemed his set apart ones; they are delivered by the blood of Christ.'

In A.D. 363 *Hilarius* wrote, 'He shall remain in the sight of God for ever, having already taken all whom he hath redeemed to be kings of heaven, and co-heirs of eternity, delivering them as the kingdom of God to the Father.'

St Ambrose tied the Father's election before creation to the Son's mission here on earth (A.D. 380): 'Before the foundation of the world, it was God's will that Christ should suffer for our salvation.'

God is just. He will not punish both the Redeemer and the redeemed. God can only collect a debt once. If someone must pay his or her own debt for sin, then clearly Jesus did not take that debt upon himself. No one for whom Christ died will be in hell, as Pacianus supports (A.D. 380): 'Much more, he will not allow him that is redeemed to be destroyed, nor will he cast away those whom he has redeemed with a great price.'

In the same vein, Ambrose asked in A.D. 380, 'Can he damn thee, whom he hath redeemed from death, for whom he offered himself, whose life he knows is the reward of his own death?'

Epiphanius annoyed some pagans when he told them that if they rejected the gospel, Christ never died for them in the first place (A.D. 390): '*If* you are redeemed ... *if* therefore ye are bought with blood ... thou art not of the number of them

who were bought with blood, O Manes, because thou deniest
the blood... He gave his life for his own sheep.'

And *Hieronymus* said, in A.D. 390, 'Christ is sacrificed for
the salvation of believers... Not all are redeemed, for not all
shall be saved, but the remnant... All those who are
redeemed and delivered by thy blood return to Zion, which
thou hast prepared for thyself by thine own blood... Christ
came to redeem Zion [a metaphor for the church] with his
blood. But lest we should think that all are Zion or every one
in Zion is truly redeemed of the Lord, who are redeemed by
the blood of Christ form the church... He did not give his life
for every man, but for many, that is, for those who would
believe.'

Anselm lost a lot of friends over this one: 'If you die in
unbelief, Christ did not die for you.'

In A.D. 850 *Remigius* reasoned, based on Scripture: 'Since
only the elect are saved, it may be accepted that Christ did not
come to save all and did not die on the cross for all.'

William Tyndale who, you will remember, was one of the
forerunners of the Reformation, was clear in his convictions
on the matter: 'Christ's blood only putteth away the sins of
them that are elect... We are elect through Christ's blood ...
Thou art elect to life everlasting by Christ's blood, whose gift
and purchase is thy faith.'

Martin Luther left little question as to where he stood on
the matter: 'For in an absolute sense, Christ did not die for
everyone, because he says: "This is my blood which is poured
out for you" and "for many" — he does not say: for every person — "for the forgiveness of sins." As the apostle says,
"Everything for the sake of the elect."'

The celebrated Anglican evangelist, *George Whitefield*,
had much to say about the definite atonement or particular
redemption of God's people. Notice his practical appeal:
'Universal redemption is a notion sadly adapted to keep the
soul in its lethargic, sleepy condition; and therefore so many

natural men admire and applaud it... Infidels of all kinds stand on the universal side of redemption: Deists, Arians, Socinians — they all arraign God's sovereignty, and stand up for universal redemption...The doctrine of universal redemption is really the highest reproach upon the dignity of the Son of God, and the merit of his blood.'

How could that be? Whitefield explains himself: 'Consider, therefore, whether it be not blasphemy to say, "Christ not only died for those that are saved, but also for those that will perish." But blessed be God, our Lord knew for whom he died.'

Again, *Charles Spurgeon*, the famous evangelist, asserts: 'Some persons love the doctrine of universal atonement... Yet if it was Christ's intention to save every man, how deplorably has he been disappointed, for there is a lake of fire, and into that pit of woe have been cast some of the very persons who, according to the theory of universal redemption, were bought with his blood... We cannot preach the gospel unless we base it upon the special and particular redemption of his elect and chosen people which Christ wrought upon the cross.'

Irresistible grace

It happens every day — whether in Los Angeles or Liverpool — no matter what the social conditions are. People undergo an internal conversion. Their views change, their disposition and interests are different. They are suddenly at peace, experiencing the deep love of God in Christ.

This event is called the new birth. It is an act of God, who tenderly and yet powerfully invades the darkness and death of the human soul, creating new life and enabling that person to respond positively in faith.

You are not 'born again' because you accept Christ; rather, you believe because the Holy Spirit has resurrected your soul and given you the gift of faith. Once alienated, stubborn, independent and rebellious — disinterested in the things of God — now you recognize your desperate need of Christ and cry out, 'Lord, be merciful to me, a sinner.'

This teaching is especially comforting when we are faced

with loved ones who appear to us to be beyond the possibility of conversion. After all, repentance is not only difficult; it's downright impossible unless it is the work of God within the individual. This point is made well by the noble father, Ignatius in A.D. 110: 'Pray for them, if so be they may repent, which is very difficult; but Jesus Christ, our true life, has the power of this.'

In that same line of thinking, *Justin Martyr* (A.D. 150) said, 'Having sometime before convinced us of the impossibility of our nature to obtain life, hath now shown us the Saviour, who is able to save them which otherwise were impossible to be saved... Free will has destroyed us; we are sold into sin.'

These thoughts confirm the impression that repentance is not a natural ability that we all possess, but rather a gift from God, given to whomever he chooses at whatever time he is pleased to grant it. Notice the earlier comment of *Barnabas* (A.D. 70) in this connection: 'God gives repentance to us, introducing us into the incorruptible temple.'

Irenæus, in A.D. 180, had this to say: 'Not of ourselves, but of God, is the blessing of our salvation... Man, who was before led captive, is taken out of the power of the possessor, according to the mercy of God the Father, and restoring it, gives salvation to it by the Word; that is, by Christ; that man may experimentally learn that not of himself, but by the gift of God, he receives immortality.'

In A.D. 200, *Tertullian* brought the debate to a simpler, more reasonable level. He asked, 'Do you think, O men, that we could ever have been able to have understood these things in the Scriptures unless by the will of him that wills all things, we had received grace to understand them? ... But by this it is plain, that it [faith] is not given to thee by God, because thou dost not ascribe it to him alone.'

The following are the words of *Cyprian* in the year A.D. 250: 'Whatsoever is grateful is to be ascribed not to man's power, but to God's gift. It is God's, I say, all is God's that we can do. Yea, that in nothing must we glory, since nothing is ours.'

Addressing himself to the heathen, *Arnobius* (A.D. 303) says, 'You place the salvation of your souls *in yourselves*, and trust that you may be made gods by your inward endeavour, yet it is not in our own power to reach things above.'

I find it interesting that in this, the third century, when Christianity was just in its elementary stages, believers nevertheless had a grasp of these teachings. After all, this same conversation between Arnobius and heathens might well have been held today with a fellow Christian. That surely is a critical sign.

In A.D. 320 *Lactantius* said rather succinctly, 'The victory lies in the will of God, not in thine own. To overcome is not in our own power.'

Athanasius, who gave his name to the foundational Athanasian Creed, said in A.D. 350, 'To believe is not ours, or in our power, but the Spirit's who is in us, and abides in us.'

Similarly, *Gregory of Nazianzum* (A.D. 370) said, 'To will is from God.'

Hieronymus said in A.D. 390, 'This is the chief righteousness of man, to reckon that whatsoever power he can have, is not his own, but the Lord's who gives it... See how great is the help of God, and how frail the condition of man that we cannot by any means fulfil this, that we repent, unless the Lord first converts us... When he [Jesus] says, "No man can come to me," he breaks the proud liberty of free will; for man can desire nothing, and in vain he endeavours... Where is the proud boasting of free will?... We pray in vain if it is in our own will. Why should men pray for that from the Lord which they have in the power of their own free will?'

In that same period, *Augustine* had made his stand for grace. In A.D. 370 he described the nature of faith and its relationship to our salvation. Obviously we do believe, that is, we make a conscious decision for or against Christ. But is that decision natural to us or must we be *first* converted before we can respond?

Augustine said, 'Faith itself is to be attributed to God... Faith is made a gift. These men, however, attribute faith to free will, so grace is rendered to faith not as a gratuitous gift, but as a debt... They must cease from saying this.'

If ever there was a man who studied the meaning of faith in the Word of God and then experienced faith radically in his own life, it must be *William Tyndale*.

Tyndale had much to say about faith. And since our misunderstanding of this doctrine is so often linked to our misconception of the nature and substance of faith, let's take a look at Tyndale's instruction on unwinding ourselves from this confused view of faith (A.D. 1520): 'Many have a certain imagination of faith. They think no farther than that faith is a thing which is in their own power to have, as do other natural works which men do... But the right faith springeth not of man's fantasy, neither is it in any man's power to obtain it; but it is altogether the pure gift of God without deserving and merits, yea, without our seeking for it, even faith is God's gift and grace... Faith rooteth herself in the hearts of the elect.

'Is it not ... perverse blindness to teach how a man can do nothing of his own self, and yet presumptuously take upon them the greatest and highest work of God, even to make faith in themselves of their own power, and of their own false imagination and thoughts?

'Therefore, I say, we must despair of ourselves and pray to God to give us faith.'

Some time later, *Martin Luther* was called onto the scene to keep the defence going for God's free and omnipotent grace: 'We become sons of God by a power divinely give us — not by any power of "free will" inherent in us! ... What is hereby attributed to man's own decision and free will? What indeed is left but nothing! In truth, nothing! Since the source of grace is the predestinating purpose of God, then it comes by necessity, and not by any effort or endeavour on our part.'

And in the nineteenth century, the 'Prince of Preachers',

Charles Spurgeon, said, 'The Holy Ghost comes, not according to our own mind or will, but according to the gift and purpose of the Lord. From top to bottom this salvation is of the Lord.'

The final perseverance of the saints

As we noted in our chapter devoted to the discussion on this subject, it is apparently unscriptural to say on the one hand, 'I'm eternally secure, no matter what I do or how I live, or what I believe,' or to say, 'If we don't keep our end up, we may lose our salvation and perish in spite of our having been redeemed.'

Rather, Scripture seems clearly to teach us that it is our responsibility to persevere in faith and conviction — with great determination even in the midst of formidable obstacles. Yet, that very perseverance is due ultimately to God's abiding grace and eternal love that will never allow us to undo what he has so graciously accomplished for us.

Clement of Rome, a contemporary of Paul's who was, as indicated earlier, mentioned in Paul's epistle to the Corinthian church, had this to say in A.D. 69: 'It is the will of God that all whom he loves should partake of repentance, and so not perish with the unbelieving and impenitent. He has established it by his almighty will. But if any of those whom God wills should partake of the grace of repentance, should afterwards perish, where is his almighty will? And how is this matter settled and established by such a will of his?'

In A.D. 190, *Clement of Alexandria* said, 'Such a soul [of a Christian] shall never at any time be separated from God... Faith, I say, is something divine, which cannot be pulled asunder by any other worldly friendship, nor be dissolved by present fear.'

That 'present fear' holds many millions of Christians in bondage today. Whereas the true gospel calls us to a present hope, this errant 'gospel' leads people to look to themselves and their own performance as a standard of hope and security in Christ.

Tertullian didn't beat around the bush on this account. He said straight out, 'God forbid that we should believe that the soul of any saint should be drawn out by the devil... For what is of God is never extinguished.'

You see, that is the central issue. If our salvation is even in some measure of ourselves, then our security depends somewhat on what we do to keep things going. If, however, salvation is of God entirely, then 'He who began a good work will complete it.' Augustine connects this grace of perseverance with that of election: 'Of these believers no one perishes, because they all were elected. And they are elected because they were called according to the purpose — the purpose, however, not their own, but God's... Obedience then is God's gift... To this, indeed, we are not able to deny, that perseverance in good, progressing even to the end, is also a great gift of God.'

God takes your salvation seriously! God loves you with an everlasting, unconditional love. That means two things: God loves you too much to see you lose the grace he has given you, and also God loves you too much to see you live a life that is inconsistent with your profession and his character. Both goals are sought and achieved by God as he works in us his good pleasure.

William Tyndale said, 'Christ is in thee, and thou in him, knit together inseparably. Neither canst thou be damned, except Christ be damned with thee: neither can Christ be saved, except thou be saved with him.'

And the eighteenth-century evangelist *George Whitefield*, added, 'A true child of God, though he might fall foully, yet could never finally fall.'

Finally, *Charles Spurgeon*, who became the leading evangelist of the following generation, left no question as to where he stood on the matter when he said, 'I cannot comprehend a gospel which lets saints fall away after they are called, and suffers the children of God to be burned in the fires of damnation after having believed in Jesus. Such a gospel I abhor.'

Credal Statements

Next we turn to the credal statements — official documents establishing the position of the Christian church on the bedrock dogmas we all hold today.

The Council of Nicæa met in A.D. 325 to define the doctrine of the Trinity. Next on the agenda was the establishment of the official position on the nature of Christ as both God and man. The Council of Chalcedon (A.D. 451) was convened for this purpose, but the issue was far from settled. Against the backdrop of this debate over the nature of Jesus Christ — utterly basic to all Christian claims — the Council of Orange was held (A.D. 529). This particular council met to establish the official Christian position on human depravity, election, the effectiveness of grace and God's sovereign prerogative. After defining this position, the church went back to the debate on the nature of Christ. Certainly these truths have played a central role in Christendom from the beginning.

The following are excerpts from Christian creeds through history, underscoring the role of these doctrines in perspective.

Council of Orange (529)

'If anyone says that the grace of God can be conferred as a result of human prayer, but that it is not grace itself which makes us pray to God, he contradicts the prophet Isaiah, or the apostle who says the same thing, "I was found by them that did not seek me; I appeared openly to them that asked not after me." If anyone maintains that God awaits our will to be cleansed from sin, but does not confess that even our will to be cleansed comes to us through the infusion and working of the Holy Spirit, he opposeth the Holy Spirit himself who says through Solomon, "The will is prepared by the Lord." If anyone says that not only the increase of faith but also its beginning and the very desire for faith, by which we believe — if anyone says that this belongs to us naturally and not by a gift of grace, that is, by the inspiration of the Holy Spirit amending our will and turning it from unbelief to faith and from godlessness to godliness, it is proof that he is opposed to the teaching of the apostles... For those who state that faith by which we believe in God is our own make all who are separated from the church of Christ in some measure believers.

'If anyone says that God has mercy upon us when, apart from his gift, we believe, will, desire, strive, labour, pray, etc., but does not confess that it is by the infusion and inspiration of the Holy Spirit within us that we even have the faith, the will, or the strength to do all these things we ought, he contradicts the apostles... If anyone affirms that we can form any right opinion or make any right choice which relates to the salvation of eternal life, or that we can be saved, that is, assent to the preaching of the gospel through our own powers ... he is led away by a heretical spirit... If anyone maintains that he comes through free will, it is proof that he has no place in the true faith.'

Council of Valence (855)

Three centuries earlier St Augustine and the monk Pelagius had battled it out over these doctrines. The teachings of Pelagius were condemned by more church councils than any other heresy in history. In the ninth century, the Catholic church was again in need of renewal and the theologian, Gottschalk, rose up to defend the doctrines of grace, though perhaps he went too far at times.

The Council of Valence reaffirmed the theology of grace and divine sovereignty: 'We confess a predestination of the elect to life, and a predestination of the wicked to death; that, in the election of those who are saved, the mercy of God precedes anything we do, and in the condemnation of those who will perish, evil merit precedes the righteous judgement of God.'

The Ten Conclusions of Berne (1528)

'God has elected us out of grace. God has from the beginning freely, and of his pure grace, without any respect of men, predestinated or elected the saints, whom he will save in Christ... We are elected or predestined in Christ. Therefore, not for any merit of ours, yet not without a means, but in Christ, and for Christ, did God choose us... We are elected to a sure end... This is therefore above all to be taught and well weighted, what great love of the Father toward us in Christ is revealed.'

The Small Catechism by Martin Luther (1529)

'I believe that by my own reason and strength I cannot believe in Jesus Christ, my Lord, or come to him. But the Holy Spirit has called me through the gospel, enlightened me with his gifts, and sanctified and preserved me in true faith, just as he calls, gathers, enlightens and sanctifies the whole Christian church on earth and preserves it in union with Jesus Christ in the one true faith... When the heavenly Father gives us his Holy Spirit so that by his grace we may believe... To be sure, the good and gracious will of God is done without our prayer, but we pray in this petition that it may also be done by *us*.'

The Augsburg Confession of the Lutheran Church (1530)

'All men are full of evil lust and inclinations from their mothers' wombs and are unable by nature to have true fear of God and true faith in God... Rejected in this connection are the Pelagians [who rejected Augustine's theology of election and grace, condemned by Orange]... For they hold that natural man is made righteous by his own powers... Without the grace and activity of the Holy Spirit man is not capable of making himself acceptable to God, of fearing God and believing in God with his whole heart... This is accomplished by the Holy Spirit.'

The Thirty-Nine Articles of the Church of England (1563)

The following excerpt is taken from the articles of doctrine upon which the Church of England is founded. The entire Anglican Communion, including American Episcopalianism, is bound by this confession: 'The condition of man after the fall of Adam is such that he cannot turn and prepare himself, by his own natural strength or good works, to faith, and calling upon God... Predestination to life is the everlasting purpose of God, whereby (before the foundations of the world were laid) he hath decreed by his counsel secret to us, to deliver from curse and damnation those whom he hath chosen in Christ out of mankind, and to bring them by Christ to everlasting salvation, as vessels made to honour... The godly consideration of predestination, and our election in Christ is full of sweet, pleasant and unspeakable comfort to godly persons... It doth greatly establish and confirm their faith of eternal salvation to be enjoyed through Christ, as because it doth fervently kindle their love towards God.'

The Westminster Confession (1646)

Earlier in the seventeenth century, kings, princes, electors and theologians had met in Dort, in the Netherlands. The great Synod of Dort convened leaders from the English church, the churches of France, Poland, Austria, Germany and other lands to reaffirm the doctrines of grace. It was at Dort that the historic 'Five Points of Calvinism' were drafted as a condemnation of the followers of Jacob Arminius, a more liberal Calvinist. Arminianism had been spreading into the churches of the Reformation, reintroducing old Roman errors that were simply recast in Protestant terms. Dort was a decisive 'No!' to Arminianism from the heirs of the Reformation. The Synod of Dort redefined total depravity, unconditional election, limited atonement, irresistible grace and perseverance of the saints (T.U.L.I.P.), and once again Augustinianism triumphed.

I have not included an excerpt from the Confession of Dort, since the entire credal statement is devoted to these doctrines.

Instead, we will jump to the latter part of the century, when the British Parliament commissioned the empire's religious leaders to come up with a confession that would bring unity to the war-torn land. The result was the Westminster Confession.

Here is an excerpt from it: 'God from all eternity did, by the most wise and holy counsel of his own will, freely and unchangeably ordain whatsoever comes to pass... By the decree of God, for the manifestation of his glory, some men and angels are predestined unto everlasting life, and others foreordained to everlasting death... Those of mankind that are predestinated unto life, God, before the foundation of the world was laid, according to his eternal and immutable purpose, and the secret counsel and good pleasure of his will, hath chosen in Christ unto everlasting glory, out of his mere free grace and love, without any foresight of faith or good works, or perseverance in either of them, or any other thing in the creature, as conditions, or causes moving him thereunto; and all to the praise of his glorious grace... Neither are any other redeemed by Christ, effectually called, justified, adopted, sanctified and saved, but the elect only.'

Confession of Dositheus (1672)

This is the most recent creed of the Eastern Orthodox Church. 'The occasion for the creed was the work of Cyril Lucaris, who had been elected Patriarch of Alexandria in 1602 and Patriarch of Constantinople [the highest position in Orthodoxy] in 1621.' Lucaris, with deep sympathies for the Reformed (Calvinist) churches in teaching 'the ancient faith', aroused the hatred of the Jesuits (a Roman Catholic order) and this creed established the modern Orthodox view, after Patriarch Lucaris had been strangled by the Turks: 'We believe the most good God to have from eternity predestined unto glory those whom he hath chosen, and to have consigned unto condemnation those whom he hath rejected.'

The Helvetic Consensus Formula (1675)

'As Christ was from eternity elected the Head, Prince and Lord of all who, in time, are saved by his grace, so also, in time, he was made surety of the New Covenant only for those who, by the eternal election, were given to him as his own people, his seed and inheritance... He encountered dreadful death in the place of the elect alone, restored only these into the bosom of the Father's grace, and these only he reconciled to God, the offended Father, and delivered from the curse of the law... The Father's election, the Son's redemption and the Spirit's sanctification is one and the same people.'

The London/Philadelphia Confession of the Baptists (1688/ 1742)

The American Baptists accepted the Philadelphia Confession in 1742, although the English Baptists had already accepted it in the Baptist creeds (1677) and the London Confession of 1688. This confession of faith is identical to the Westminster Confession, except on matters related to the sacraments. The purpose was to show the world the common agreement of all Christians on these doctrines of grace.

The New Hampshire Confession of The Baptists in America (1833)

'We believe that election is the gracious purpose of God, according to which he graciously regenerates, sanctifies and saves sinners ... that it is a most glorious display of God's sovereign goodness ... that it excludes boasting, and promotes humility, love, prayer, praise, trust in God, and active imitation of his free mercy ... that it is the foundation of Christian assurance; and that to ascertain it with regard to ourselves demands and deserves our utmost diligence.'

Abstract of Principles (1859)

This creed was first drawn up for the Southern Baptist denomination and its schools. It is still endorsed and accepted officially by the denomination.

'Election is God's eternal choice of some persons unto everlasting life — not because of foreseen merit in them, but of his mere mercy in Christ — in consequence of which choice they are called, justified and glorified... The Son lives to make intercession for his people... Regeneration is a change of heart, wrought by the Holy Spirit, who quickeneth the dead in trespasses and sins, enlightening their minds spiritually and savingly to understand the Word of God... It is a work of God's free and special grace alone.'

Conclusion

In drawing together the scriptural quotations, the attestations from the fathers and heroes of the faith, and the credal statements, my problem throughout has been how to edit and limit the material to a convenient size. Needless to say, such a wealth of material from Scripture and tradition gives unity of support to the truths of God's free grace.

It becomes clear from this study that whenever the church affirms and proclaims this message, it awakens to the world and reawakens the world to God's activity. The creeds show that the Baptists, Presbyterians, Lutherans, Anglicans and Episcopalians, Congregationalists, Roman Catholics (in spite of the Council of Trent and more recent statements), Eastern Orthodox churches and other bodies are all historically founded upon these truths. And the great heroes of our faith, the people who were used by God to usher us into the brightest eras of history, lived and breathed these themes. The Scriptures are the divine depository of these rich teachings and emphasize them with crystal-clear definition.

In the light of all this, we can have good reason to expect to see a new glorious dawning on the horizon if we will only once again confess our faith in the Alpha and Omega of creation and salvation. Should we choose to remain in ignorance and apathy, the world will continue to sing other men's songs.

Let us work, for the hour is late! Amen.

References

Chapter 1
1. Daniel Thrapp, *The Choice of Truth*, quoted in *The Encyclopedia of Religious Quotations*, Frank S. Mead, ed., Revell, 1976, p. 677.
2. Paul C. Payne, *The Encyclopedia of Religious Quotations*, p. 124.
3. Eugene F. Rice, Jr, *The Foundations of Early Modern Europe*, W. W. Norton & Co., Inc., 1970, p. 136.

Chapter 2
1. Harold Kushner, *When Bad Things Happen to Good People*, Avon Books, 1981, pp. 42-3.
2. As above, p. 46.
3. Sir John Eccles, 'Science Can't Explain...' *US News and World Report*, February 1985.
4. As above.

Chapter 3
1. Robert Rosenblatt, 'What Really Matters?', *Time*, October 1983, pp. 24-7.

Chapter 4
1. D. James Kennedy, *Truths That Transform*, Revell, 1974.

Chapter 5
1. James Daane, *The Freedom of God*, William B. Eerdmans, 1973, p. 14.
2. Dietrich Bonhoeffer, *The Cost of Discipleship*, Macmillan, 1963, pp. 45, 47.
3. Martin Luther, *Bondage of the Will*, trans. by Henry Cole, Baker Books, 1976, pp. 217.
4. John R. W. Stott, *God's New Society*, InterVarsity Press, 1982.

Chapter 6
1. John Boys, quoted in *The Golden Treasury of Puritan Quotations*, compiled by I. D. E. Thomas, Banner of Truth, 1977, p. 47.

Chapter 7
1. Lewis Sperry Chafer, 'For Whom Did Christ Die?' *Bibliotheca Sacra*, October-December 1980, p. 325.

Chapter 9
1.   Benjamin B. Warfield, *The Plan of Salvation*, reprinted, William B. Eerdmans, 1980, p. 95.
2.   Robert Lightner, 'For Whom Did Christ Die?' in *Tribute to Walvoord*, Moody Press, 1982, p. 162.
3.   Norman Geisler, 'God, Evil, and Dispensation' in *Tribute to Walvoord*, pp. 102-3.
4.   A. W. Tozer, *The Best of Tozer*, Baker Books, 1980, p. 175.
5.   Stott, *God's New Society*.
6.   Luther, *Bondage of the Will*, p. 36.
7.   Kennedy, *Truths That Transform*, pp. 39-40.
8.   Will Metzger, *Tell the Truth*, InterVarsity Press, 1981.

Chapter 11
1.   George Gallup, Jr, *Search for America's Faith*, Abingdon, 1984.
2.   Pat Robertson, 'The American Church at the Crossroads,' *Christian Herald,* March 1985, pp. 22-4.

Chapter 12
1.   Luther, *Bondage of the Will,* p. 70.

More titles from
Evangelical Press

Son of Mary, Son of God

What the Bible teaches about the person of Christ

Stuart Olyott

The Lord Jesus Christ is the centre of true Christianity. Yet so often the glorious truths about the person of Christ are degraded either by the false teaching of cults or by a lack of biblical instruction in the church.

Stuart Olyott answers this confusion with a clear and simple presentation of the scriptural teaching on Christ, portraying him in all his human nature and divine glory as both Son of Mary and Son of God.

Here is a book that will deepen our understanding of the person of Christ and cause us to fall afresh at his feet in a spirit of praise and worship.

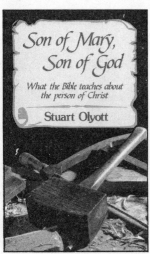

The Three are One
What the Bible teaches about the Trinity

Stuart Olyott

To deny that Jesus Christ is God is to deny a fundamental truth of the Bible. Yet it is at this point that many of the cults differ from Scripture. Every true Christian believes that the three Persons of the Godhead – Father, Son and Holy Spirit – are three yet one. How do we understand the Bible's teaching on the Trinity and how can we refute those who reject the truth?

Stuart Olyott shows that the fact of theTrinity is clearly taught in Scripture and that it is foundational to the Christian gospel. In straightforward language the author seeks to lead the reader to a better understanding of what God has revealed about himself.